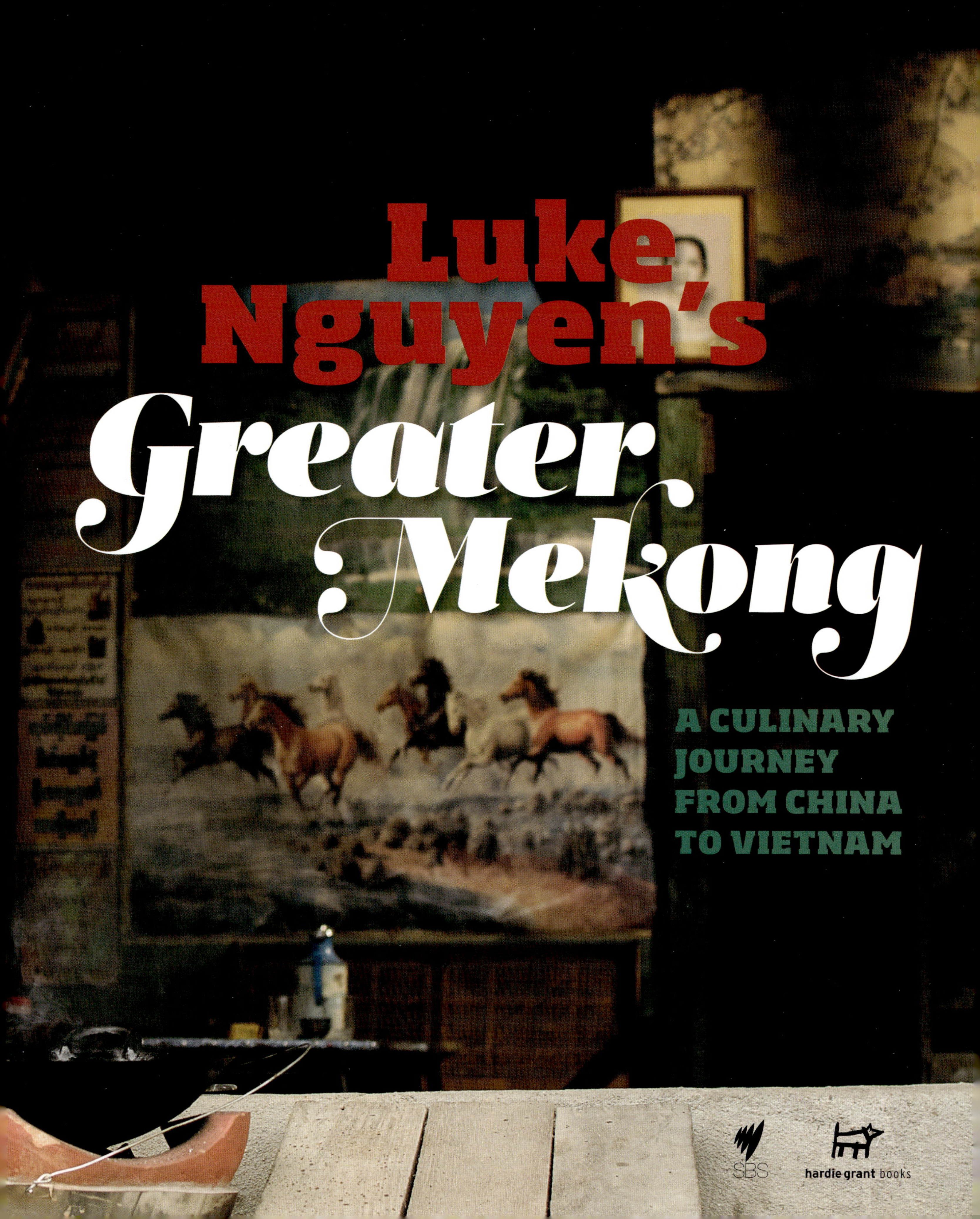

Luke Nguyen's Greater Mekong

A CULINARY JOURNEY FROM CHINA TO VIETNAM

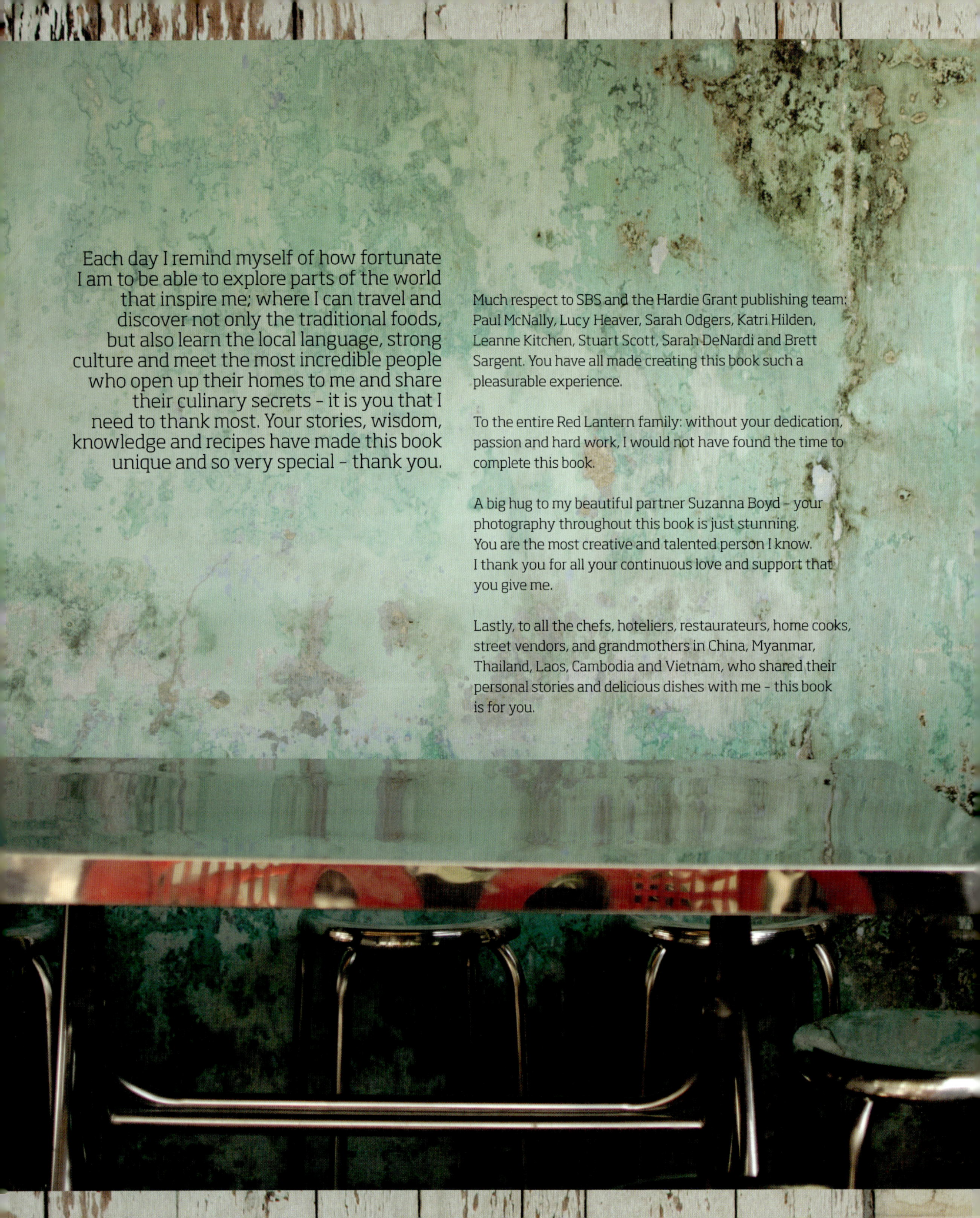

Each day I remind myself of how fortunate I am to be able to explore parts of the world that inspire me; where I can travel and discover not only the traditional foods, but also learn the local language, strong culture and meet the most incredible people who open up their homes to me and share their culinary secrets – it is you that I need to thank most. Your stories, wisdom, knowledge and recipes have made this book unique and so very special – thank you.

Much respect to SBS and the Hardie Grant publishing team: Paul McNally, Lucy Heaver, Sarah Odgers, Katri Hilden, Leanne Kitchen, Stuart Scott, Sarah DeNardi and Brett Sargent. You have all made creating this book such a pleasurable experience.

To the entire Red Lantern family: without your dedication, passion and hard work, I would not have found the time to complete this book.

A big hug to my beautiful partner Suzanna Boyd – your photography throughout this book is just stunning. You are the most creative and talented person I know. I thank you for all your continuous love and support that you give me.

Lastly, to all the chefs, hoteliers, restaurateurs, home cooks, street vendors, and grandmothers in China, Myanmar, Thailand, Laos, Cambodia and Vietnam, who shared their personal stories and delicious dishes with me – this book is for you.

CONTENTS

INTRODUCTION 6

CHINA 12
- KUNMING 18
- DALI & SHAXI 26
- LIJIANG 42
- XISHUANGBANNA 54

MYANMAR 64
- YANGON 70
- INLE LAKE 80
- KENGTUNG 92

THAILAND 106
- CHIANG KHONG 112
- MAE SALONG 124
- CHIANG MAI 134

LAOS 146
- VIENTIANE 152
- LUANG PRABANG 164
- 4000 ISLANDS 182

CAMBODIA 188
- SIEM REAP 194
- PHNOM PENH 204
- KEP & KAMPOT 214

VIETNAM 230
- CHAU DOC 236
- CAI BE 246
- BEN TRE 256

GLOSSARY 264
INDEX 267

Introduction

Vietnam is a country I have been returning to for the past ten years, to deepen my understanding of its culture and its diverse regional cuisine. On each visit I would spend my days visiting home cooks, street vendors and cottage industries, from the northern mountains of Sapa through to the cosmopolitan city of Saigon, then further south to the Mekong Delta, visiting my uncles, aunties and cousins who live right on the banks of the Mekong River.

We would wake early in the mornings and jump straight into the river to freshen up. The women would then spend most of the day harvesting rice from the green paddies, while the men fished for mudfish, tilapia and snakehead fish, and children picked plump succulent mangoes, jackfruit, lychees and durian from the orchards. All the produce was then packed onto longboats to begin the eight-hour journey up the Mekong to the wholesale markets in Saigon.

My family's entire livelihood revolved around the Mekong. This abundant river irrigated their rice crops and fruit orchards, supplied hundreds of kilos of fish each day and was their main means of transport.

I began to appreciate how many Vietnamese families along the Mekong Delta rely solely on the river to survive. It was then I realised that it isn't simply the people of Vietnam who depend on the mighty Mekong to sustain their lives.

The Mekong is the twelfth longest river in the world, and the heart and soul of mainland South-East Asia. Over 60 million people depend on the river and its tributaries for food, water, transport and many other aspects of their daily lives. The river also supports one of the world's most diverse fisheries, nurturing over 1500 different species of fish within its vast ecosystem.

I decided to embark on a journey to explore the many countries along the Mekong that use the river every day for nourishment and life. I wanted to immerse myself in the culture and lifestyles of the people in the Greater Mekong region and learn of the incredibly diverse produce, ingredients and cuisines of these areas.

My discovery of the Greater Mekong starts where the mighty river begins its flow from the Tibetan Plateau, making its way down to China's Yunnan Province – the most ethnically diverse region in China. I explore the culinary cultures and centuries-old traditions and stories of the Yunnan, from the Naxi people of Lijiang to the Dai communities of Xishuangbanna.

Journeying south to Myanmar, I uncover the unique flavours of the former capital, Yangon. I meet the friendliest and most hospitable people that I have ever encountered, and learn the family recipes of Inle Lake communities and cook with the hill tribes of the Shan State.

I then cross the border into northern Thailand. Beginning in Chiang Khong, and then in Mae Salong and Chiang Mai, I learn from local fishermen, home cooks and Akha grandmothers that the mighty Mekong River is more than just a source of food – it is a way of life.

My journey continues down the lower Mekong to Laos, where I discover unusual ingredients and unique dishes that surprise my senses. I start in the country's capital, Vientiane, where I glean a better understanding of the cuisine, and the many influences that have shaped it to become the 'next big flavour' to hit the Western world. I then visit the nation's food capital, Luang Prabang, where I experience the seven-day celebrations of the Lao New Year, and sample the wonderful street food this charming colonial town has to offer.

I travel further south to 4000 Islands, where the Mekong River spills across and around a giant expanse of rocks, rapids and islands on its way down to Cambodia. This stunning area has some of the most unusual fish and insect dishes in the country.

As I cross over to Cambodia, I am overwhelmed by the people's stories, resilience, and their passion for their cuisine and culture. Throughout the country, beginning in Siem Reap, I meet inspiring cooks who are striving to bring back ancient Khmer food and put their cuisine back on the world map.

Further south, I arrive in the capital, Phnom Penh, where in just a few moments one can see and feel the true Cambodia: the contradictory contrast of the old and new, poor and rich, harsh and kind, honest and corrupt. In Phnom Penh I sample everything from rustic street food to high-end dining, but what stays true is the authenticity of Khmer cuisine.

The Mekong River flows further south through Cambodia to Kep and Kampot, known to have the best crab, squid and green peppercorns in all of South-East Asia.

A simple short walk across some white lines and a boom gate, and I'm in my mother country, Vietnam. Here I travel with my parents, digging deeper, wanting to learn more about the lives of the Vietnamese people along the Mekong Delta. We start in Chau Doc, where I sample the world-class fermented fish and the country's best roast suckling pig.

I continue by boat to Cai Be, where river meets land, to visit the colourful vibrant floating markets, and spend time at local cottage industries learning age-old cooking techniques.

My Greater Mekong adventure sadly ends in Ben Tre, where I am taught everything there is to know about the coconut tree. And it is in Ben Tre that I am initiated by the locals, coaxed into eating mice and live coconut worms, finally becoming a true Vietnamese man.

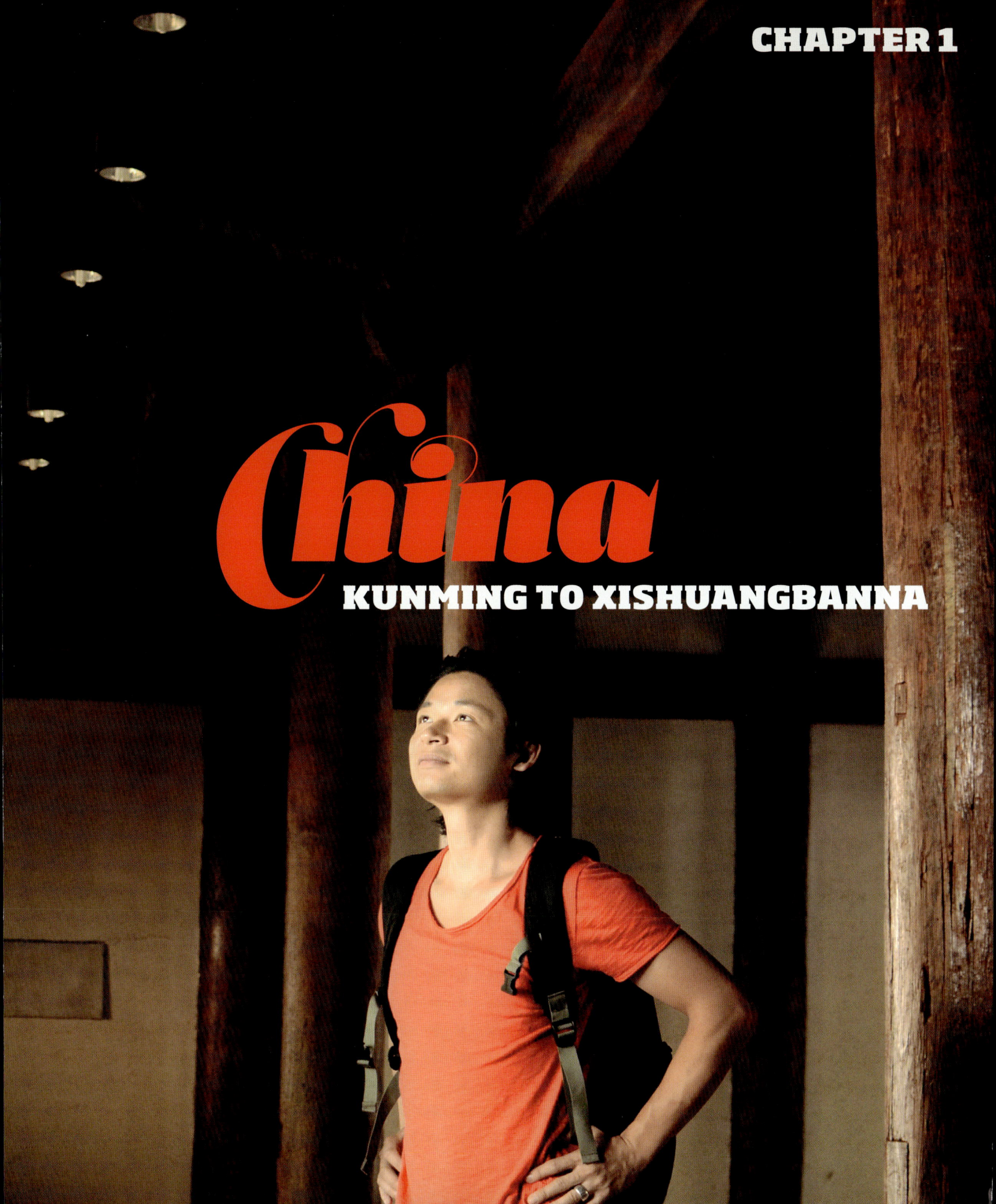

China
KUNMING TO XISHUANGBANNA

Of all the countries I've visited in Asia, it is the people of China who have impressed me most with their knowledge of and reverence for their regional food specialties. I witnessed many passionate debates about food and ingredients, and learnt that in the story of food, you'll also find the stories of love, war, deceit, comedy, tragedy, triumph and celebration. With such a rich and long history, it is little wonder China remains such a master of Asian cuisine.

One of the many things I love about China is its tradition of storytelling, which holds little gems of history and memories of times past.

By discovering a dish or item of produce, I'd often uncover with it a story dating back centuries – a wonderful way of keeping the past locked into the present, and recognising history in the everyday food that is still grown and traded.

I'd felt a lot of pressure starting to film this new cooking series in China, as I couldn't speak the language, and the ethnic cuisines in this vast country are so different from what we know of in the West as 'Chinese' – a huge contrast for me to Vietnam where, in comparison, I'd felt protected and comfortable within my own heritage and language.

China, to me, is the grandmother of all Asian cuisines, and the source of so many other Asian 'ways' and authenticities.

Every day in China, I would learn of new medicinal herbs, spices, green vegetables, oils, cooking techniques and flavours. Meeting the people and wandering through the markets would take me on an exciting culinary journey, educating me about 'real' Chinese cooking and ingredients. I immersed myself so deeply in the culture, eating everything on offer and doing my best to speak the language, that I began to feel like a local.

I started my journey in the Yunnan capital, Kunming, affectionately known as the City of Eternal Spring, where I discovered the iconic dishes and old-world stories of this great metropolis.

Yunnan province in southern China is the most ethnically diverse area in the country. It is also the region that has long been known as 'Shangri La' – the remote, mythical long-lost paradise on earth. The landscape here is dramatic and beautiful, and home to interesting and sometimes rare ingredients.

I then made my way to the Dali and Shaxi regions, where I discovered the unique culinary flavours and traditions of the Bai and Yi people, and spent time along the historic 'Tea Horse Trail'.

From there I took a long drive to the fabled old town of Lijiang, where I met up with a Naxi family who kindly taught me their local specialties.

My trip in China wound up in Xishuangbanna, the gateway to South-East Asia, where I experienced the Dai culture and cuisine.

It was a fascinating journey indeed.

THE GLOWING LIGHTS OF NIGHT KIOSKS OFFER KUNMING-STYLE VERSIONS OF THE FAITHFUL HAMBURGER

CHINA

Kunming is known as the City of Eternal Spring, as the air is clean and crisp, and the soil is very fertile. Most of China's flowers, fresh herbs and vegetables are grown here, and that's what I'd come to explore. Kunming feels at ease merging the new with the old, perhaps because of its youthful population of university students, who are ever adapting and evolving with all the new fashions and technology.

Kunming

Since my first visit to Kunming, over seven years ago, the city has become modernised: electric motorbikes and cars fill the streets and, for the first time ever, the road rules are actually obeyed, and street-food vendors, who once offered delicious Muslim and Chinese snacks, can no longer trade wherever they feel like on the streets.

My flight arrived early in the morning, so I made my way to the Golden Horse Gates in the centre of town, where I watched hundreds of elderly ladies exercising and dancing in the public square, following traditional old moves set to contemporary music. I couldn't help but join in.

Afterwards, the ladies told me of a favourite local dish called 'crossing the bridge noodles'. Like so many dishes in China, this noodle soup had history (see page 23). They pointed out a restaurant called Brothers Jiang that had been serving this dish for 60 years. When a dish has a great story behind it, I have to say it adds so much more to the dining experience.

After breakfast I was already thinking about lunch, so I asked people on the streets what I should eat and where. A university student told me of a hidden laneway where I could find the best chargrilled halal beef skewers, cooked by a guy named Mr Shwee. He is part of the largest minority group in China, the Uyghur people – also known as Muslim Chinese. They are famous for their skewers, but because this popular street food is now illegal, only the best cooks remain, hidden from public sight.

The next day, I drove to the Stone Forest, where 400,000 square kilometres of limestone karsts have been skilfully sculpted by nature over the past 200 million years. But first I had to visit one of the best roast duck restaurants in China, in the town of Yiliang, where master chef Pan has been roasting duck for 25 years. He marinates the ducks, then air-dries them for 24 hours, ensuring a lovely crisp skin. They are then cooked over burning dried pine needles, giving them an amazing smoky rosemary aroma. It was better than the roast duck in Beijing everyone raves about!

INGREDIENTS

250 g (9 oz) firm tofu, drained
60 ml (2 fl oz/¼ cup) vegetable oil
200 g (7 oz) fish mint root (glossary), cut into 3 cm (1¼ inch) lengths
1 handful fish mint leaves (glossary)
1 large handful mint leaves
1 small handful roughly chopped coriander (cilantro)
8 garlic chives, roughly chopped
¼ red capsicum (pepper), finely sliced

DRESSING

2 teaspoons brown sugar
1 tablespoon Chinese black vinegar
1½ tablespoons light soy sauce
½ teaspoon sesame oil
pinch of chilli flakes
2 small garlic cloves, finely chopped
2.5 cm (1 inch) piece of fresh ginger, finely sliced
1 spring onion (scallion), finely sliced

FISH MINT ROOT & TOFU SALAD

SERVES 4 as part of a shared meal

Eating in Kunming was such an incredible learning experience. Every day, I sampled something new and unique.

On my very first day I was introduced to an unusual ingredient called 'zheergen', which is the root of the fish mint. Its name comes from its flavour, which is definitely an acquired taste. It's a bit fishy and quite astringent, but I loved it.

Locals say this pale, spindly, crunchy root was their natural prevention against severe acute respiratory syndrome, or SARS.

If you can't get your hands on fish mint root, use cooked, julienned young bamboo shoots or lotus stems instead.

METHOD

Combine the dressing ingredients in a mixing bowl and stir until the sugar has dissolved. Set aside and allow the flavours to infuse for 10 minutes.

Meanwhile, cut the tofu into large cubes. Heat the vegetable oil in a small saucepan and fry the tofu over medium heat for 4–5 minutes, turning until browned on all sides.

Remove the tofu with a slotted spoon and place in a large mixing bowl. Add the remaining salad ingredients and the dressing and toss well.

Transfer to a platter and serve.

INGREDIENTS

cooked chicken, from the chicken stock (see below)
100 g (3½ oz) boneless, skinless chicken breast, sliced paper thin
100 g (3½ oz) skinless pork fillet, sliced paper thin
40 g (1½ oz) pork kidney, peeled, trimmed and sliced paper thin
50 g (2 oz) Chinese cured pork (glossary) or jamón, finely sliced
100 g (3½ oz) cleaned squid, sliced paper thin
1 sheet of dried tofu skin (glossary), soaked in water for 20 minutes, then finely sliced
100 g (3½ oz) fresh black fungus (wood ears; glossary), sliced
1 handful Pickled Vegetables (page 212), optional, roughly chopped
2 spring onions (scallions), finely sliced
6 baby bok choy (pak choy) leaves, cut into 3 cm (1¼ inch) strips
4 garlic chives, cut into 3 cm (1¼ inch) lengths
1 small handful chopped coriander (cilantro), plus extra to garnish
300 g (10½ oz) fresh round Chinese rice noodles
1 quail egg
½ teaspoon sea salt
1 tablespoon soy sauce
1 teaspoon finely sliced fresh ginger

CHICKEN STOCK

1 kg (2 lb 3 oz) whole chicken
3 garlic cloves
4 spring onions (scallions), white part only, roughly chopped
4 cm (1½ inch) piece of fresh ginger, peeled and sliced

CROSSING THE BRIDGE NOODLES
SERVES 4

METHOD

First, prepare the chicken stock. Wash the chicken thoroughly under cold running water, being sure to remove all traces of blood, guts and fat from the cavity. Place the chicken in a stockpot with 3 litres (102 fl oz/12 cups) water and bring to the boil.

Reduce the heat to a slow simmer and skim off any impurities. Continue to skim until you have removed most of the fat. Pound the garlic and spring onion into a paste using a mortar and pestle, then add to the pot with the ginger. Cook for a further 2 hours. Strain off the stock, reserving the chicken carcass, and allow the stock to cool. Pour off and reserve 1 litre (34 fl oz/4 cups) of the stock; refrigerate the remaining stock for up to 3 days and use in other recipes, or freeze until required.

Finely shred the meat from the chicken carcass, discarding the skin and bones, and place on a small plate. Arrange the sliced meats, squid, tofu, vegetables, herbs and noodles on separate small plates. Crack the egg into a small bowl and place on the serving table with all the food plates.

Bring the reserved stock to the boil with the salt, soy sauce and ginger. Allow to boil briefly, as the broth must be boiling hot.

Transfer the broth to a very large warmed noodle bowl and bring to the serving table.

Quickly add the egg to the boiling broth, followed by the meats, squid, and then the remaining ingredients, adding the noodles last.

Combine well, and distribute among individual warmed bowls. Garnish with extra coriander and serve.

Kunming's most renowned dish has its origins in a beautiful Chinese story. Centuries ago, a scholar would go to a small island to study for the Imperial exams. Every day, his loving wife would bring him lunch, but to reach him she had to cross a bridge, so her soups were always cold. Then she came up with an idea! She sliced all the soup ingredients super thin, used a huge bowl to hold her piping-hot broth and poured a layer of fat on top, to trap the heat. She would then carry the hot soup over the bridge, with all the ingredients on separate plates. Only when she reached her husband did she assemble the soup, and as everything was so finely sliced, the ingredients cooked very quickly in the steaming broth. Legend says her husband did very well in his exams.

INGREDIENTS

1 kg (2 lb 3 oz) beef sirloin
125 ml (4 fl oz/½ cup) vegetable oil
1 teaspoon chilli flakes
1 teaspoon ground cumin
2 lemons, cut into wedges

MARINADE

3 teaspoons sea salt
1 teaspoon sweet paprika
1 teaspoon ground nutmeg
1 teaspoon ground coriander
1 teaspoon ground sichuan peppercorns
1 teaspoon ground ginger
1 teaspoon chilli flakes
1 teaspoon ground cumin
3 garlic cloves, finely chopped
60 ml (2 fl oz/¼ cup) light soy sauce
60 ml (2 fl oz/¼ cup) vegetable oil

UYGHUR SPICY BEEF SKEWERS

MAKES 12 (SERVES 4)

The Uyghur are one of China's largest ethnic minorities. In Kunming they are known for their Chinese-Muslim cuisine – especially for their beef or lamb skewers, cooked on the streets over glowing charcoal. Sadly, street food in Kunming is fast disappearing, as the local government has been cracking down on street vendors.

However, I heard of a cook named Mr Shwee, whose family has been serving beef skewers for three generations. I had a hard time finding him: he hides his charcoal grill down a narrow alley, out of police view. His recipe is as secret as his location! I tried my best to replicate his marinade, and I think I'm almost there … Mr Shwee grills some 2000 skewers a day, for 3 yuan per stick, making $700 per day. Not bad, hey?

METHOD

Combine the marinade ingredients in a bowl and mix well.

Cut the beef into 2.5 cm (1 inch) chunks, leaving on some of the fat. Place in a large mixing bowl, add the marinade and mix until the beef is well coated. Cover and marinate in the refrigerator for at least 30 minutes, or overnight for a tastier result.

Soak 12 bamboo skewers in cold water for 20 minutes. Heat a barbecue chargrill or chargrill pan to medium-high heat.

Thread the beef onto the skewers. Chargrill for 3 minutes on each side, basting the beef with the vegetable oil to get some flame happening and impart a smoky flavour, and sprinkling with the chilli flakes and cumin.

Transfer to a platter and serve with lemon wedges.

CHINA

The rural town of Dali was settled by the Bai people 3000 years ago. About 300 kilometres north-west of Kunming, Dali is the economic and cultural centre of the Dali Bai Autonomous Prefecture. The area is surrounded by mountains to the east, west and south, with Erhai Lake in its centre. Here you will find 25 ethnic minorities, who have created a unique culture and cuisine.

Dali & Shaxi

Dali is famous for its rice noodles, which have a unique sticky texture. I arranged to spend a day with a family who has been making rice noodles for four generations.
I was greeted at the door of an old wooden house by the Zhao family, wearing their traditional colourful Bai garb and pink headpieces.

I arrived in time to see huge baskets of soaked rice being steamed. The rice – a mixture of jasmine and glutinous rice – is steamed for 40 minutes, rested and steamed again. It is then kneaded into a thick dough, rolled flat, then hung on wooden beams for 24 hours. The whole family then cut the noodles with large cleavers. They were true artisans; I felt like I had stepped back in time. The end result was the most incredible 'al dente noodles' I have ever tried. If only we could get such fresh hand-made rice noodles at home.

Noodle-making is not the only tradition in Dali dating back hundreds of years. Sitting in a tiny boat listening to Bai fishermen communicating with cormorants, telling the birds when to dive for fish and when to come back, was like watching theatre, or even a musical: the birds' cries and their masters' voices merging together like a wonderful song.

Located halfway between Dali and Lijiang, nestled deep in the Himalayan foothills, Shaxi is home to a beautiful traditional way of life that offers a glimpse into a forgotten era. Shaxi is a charming small town with a sun-drenched, fertile plain that follows the gentle Heihui River, a lesser-known branch of the Mekong.

Elder Bai and Yi people live here surrounded by cobbled streets, spectacular ancient architecture and impressive courtyard homes. The younger generations have all moved to the cities, so all you can do in Shaxi is go for short walks, relax and prepare 'slow' food. I really enjoyed learning dishes from the elders: you can glean so much about their culture, traditions and family values from their food.

Genghis Khan's grandson came to Dali and conquered the Dali Kingdom. These people brought their own style of food to Dali, and this 700-year-old soup is a classic example. It is much more savoury than your traditional spicy-sour-style Chinese soup, as it is more meaty and rich flavours dominate. I really enjoy using a clay pot, as it develops flavour with age and adds an earthy character to dishes. If you are using a new clay pot for the first time, submerge it in cold water overnight before cooking in it, so it doesn't crack when placed over high heat.

INGREDIENTS

2 tablespoons peanut oil
1 teaspoon sichuan peppercorns
4 cm (1½ inch) piece of fresh ginger, peeled and julienned
700 g (1 lb 9 oz) whole carp or silver perch, cleaned and butterflied
2 Chinese cabbage leaves, cut into 3 cm (1¼ inch) wide strips
40–50 g (1½–2 oz) bundle of glass noodles, soaked in water for 20 minutes
20 g (¾ oz/1 cup) dried black fungus (wood ears; glossary)
3 fresh shiitake mushrooms, sliced
40 g (1½ oz/1 cup) dried tofu skin (glossary), soaked in water for 20 minutes, then sliced quite finely
1 tablespoon dried shrimp (glossary)
10 cm (4 inch) piece of Chinese cured pork (glossary), finely sliced
fresh or dried day lily buds (glossary), to garnish, optional

CLAY POT FISH

SERVES 4 as part of a shared meal

METHOD

Add the peanut oil to a hot frying pan. Sauté the sichuan peppercorns and ginger over medium-high heat until fragrant.

Place the fish skin side down in the pan and cook for 2 minutes. Turn it over and cook for a further 2 minutes.

Place the cabbage in a 1 litre (34 fl oz/4 cup) clay pot, then transfer the pan ingredients to the clay pot.

Place the clay pot on the stove and pour in enough water to fill the pot. Bring the liquid to the boil, then skim off any impurities that rise to the surface.

Add the noodles, mushrooms, tofu skin, dried shrimp and pork. Reduce the heat to low and simmer gently for 30 minutes.

Serve garnished with lily buds, if desired.

INGREDIENTS

700 g (1 lb 9 oz) whole carp, barramundi or silver perch, cleaned
35 g (1¼ oz/¼ cup) sea salt, for coating
40–50 g (1½–2 oz) bundle of glass noodles, soaked in water for 20 minutes
2 teaspoons fermented soya beans (glossary)
4 cm (1½ inch) piece of fresh ginger, peeled and julienned
4 spring onions (scallions), shredded
1 long red chilli, sliced
2 tablespoons peanut oil
coriander (cilantro) leaves, to garnish

SAUCE

1 tablespoon sugar
2 tablespoons shaoxing rice wine (glossary)
60 ml (2 fl oz/¼ cup) light soy sauce
1 tablespoon sesame oil

STEAMED FISH WITH FERMENTED SOYA BEANS & GLASS NOODLES

SERVES 4 as part of a shared meal

I'd heard stories of an age-old fishing technique, dating back to 960 AD, of Bai Chinese fishermen training cormorants to dive into the water to catch and retrieve fish. I could hardly believe they still do this today. It was like theatre: the communication, trust and undivided attention between the fishermen and cormorants was amazing to see.
When I finally succeeded in taking a fish out of a bird's mouth, I decided to steam the whole fish on the small canoe, with ten cormorants watching me like hawks – an experience I will never forget …
Steaming is such a simple, clean, healthy way of cooking fish. Make sure the water is at a rapid boil before cooking it.

METHOD

Make three long diagonal cuts in the thickest part on both sides of the fish. Rub sea salt over the fish, then place it on a heatproof plate that will fit inside a large steamer basket. Top with the noodles, soya beans and ginger. Set aside.

Half-fill a steamer, wok or large saucepan with water and bring to a rapid boil over high heat.

Combine the sauce ingredients in a small bowl and mix until the sugar has dissolved. Pour the sauce over the fish.

Place the fish in a steamer basket, then cover and set over the pan of boiling water. Steam for 10–15 minutes, or until the fish flakes easily when tested with a fork. Scatter the spring onion and chilli over the fish.

Heat the peanut oil in a small saucepan to smoking hot. Pour it over the fish, scalding the spring onion and chilli and releasing a fragrant, smoky, nutty aroma. Garnish with coriander and serve.

INGREDIENTS

2 tablespoons Garlic Water (see Note)
2 tablespoons peanut oil
2 garlic cloves, finely chopped
90 g (3 oz/2 cups) sliced Chinese cabbage
120 g (4 oz/1⅓ cups) bean sprouts
8 garlic chives, cut into 3 cm (1¼ inch) lengths
1 tablespoon light soy sauce
250 g (9 oz) fresh round Chinese rice noodles
½ teaspoon Vietnamese pickled ground chillies (glossary)
2 spring onions (scallions), sliced on the diagonal

YUNNAN CHILLI OIL

125 ml (4 fl oz/½ cup) peanut oil
2 tablespoons chilli flakes
1 tablespoon sesame oil

DALI VEGETARIAN RICE NOODLE STIR-FRY

SERVES 4 as part of a shared meal

China invented noodles over 4000 years ago, and when I met the Zhao family in Dali I was in noodle heaven! They've been making rice noodles for four generations, but what makes theirs so unique is that they use a mixture of jasmine rice and white glutinous rice, giving the noodles a wonderful 'al dente' texture.

METHOD

Make the garlic water a day ahead. Set aside.

You can also make the yunnan chilli oil ahead of time. Heat the peanut oil in a wok until it almost reaches smoking point. Turn off the heat and allow the oil to cool for about 3 minutes. Place the chilli flakes in a glass jar, then pour in the hot oil, followed by the sesame oil. Allow to cool slightly before sealing; do not strain or discard the chilli. The oil will keep for up to a month stored in a cool, dark place and can be used in other noodle recipes.

Heat a wok or large frying pan until smoking. Add the peanut oil and sauté the garlic over medium–high heat until fragrant. Now add the cabbage, bean sprouts and garlic chives and stir-fry for 1 minute.

Add 1 teaspoon of the yunnan chilli oil, the soy sauce and a pinch of sea salt and stir-fry for a further minute. Next add the noodles, pickled ground chillies, garlic water and half the spring onion. Stir-fry for another 3 minutes.

Transfer to a platter or individual plates, garnish with the remaining spring onion and serve.

NOTE

To make garlic water, simply combine 1 tablespoon chopped garlic and 2 tablespoons water in a bowl. Cover and stand overnight, then strain.

CHINA — DALI & SHAXI

NESTLED DEEP IN THE HIMALAYAN FOOTHILLS, SHAXI IS HOME TO A BEAUTIFULLY PRESERVED WAY OF LIFE THAT OFFERS A GLIMPSE INTO A FORGOTTEN ERA

INGREDIENTS

150 g (5 oz/2 cups) fresh lichen or fresh black fungus (wood ear; glossary), cut in half
2 whole dried Chinese white fungus (glossary), soaked in water for 30 minutes, then sliced
1 small handful roughly chopped coriander (cilantro)

DRESSING

1 tablespoon brown sugar
1 tablespoon Chinese red vinegar (glossary)
2 tablespoons Chinese black vinegar
60 ml (2 fl oz/¼ cup) light soy sauce
2 teaspoons sesame oil
3 garlic cloves, finely chopped
4 cm (1½ inch) piece of fresh ginger, peeled and finely sliced
2 spring onions (scallions), finely sliced
½ teaspoon chilli flakes

LICHEN SALAD
SERVES 4 as part of a shared meal

Shaxi's landscape was so stunning, and the air so crisp, that I promptly borrowed a bicycle and cruised around the charming old town and countryside. What took my eye were two ladies skilfully carving something from a tree. It was fresh lichen – an astonishing partnership between two very different organisms, fungus and alga. Lichen inhabit just about any solid surface in less extreme climates, from rocks and walls to trees and concrete. A few are unattached and blow about freely.

Once known as a peasant food, lichen is now a delicacy. Locals tell me it's their secret to living past the age of 90 years. I am 'lichen' the sound of that ...

METHOD

Combine the dressing ingredients in a mixing bowl and stir until the sugar has dissolved. Set aside and allow the flavours to infuse for 10 minutes.

Place the remaining ingredients in a large mixing bowl. Add the dressing and toss well.

Transfer to a platter and serve.

There is a very traditional banquet cooked in the charming town of Shaxi, called the 'Eight Dish Banquet', which is only prepared on very special occasions.

A town elder found an original banquet menu from 90 years ago and talked me through the dishes. He tells me that the red braised pork belly was one of his favourites as it was not only delicious, but, being red in colour, always brought good luck. If you can't find red rice grains, you can use 1 tablespoon Annatto Oil (see Note, page 241), or a dash of red food colouring instead.

LUCKY RED BRAISED PORK BELLY

SERVES 4 as part of a shared meal

INGREDIENTS
1 tablespoon red rice grains (hong qu; glossary)
1 tablespoon shaoxing rice wine (glossary)
500 g (1 lb 2 oz) boneless pork belly, cut into 3 cm x 4 cm (1¼ inch x 1½ inch) pieces
2 teaspoons sugar
5 cm (2 inch) piece of fresh ginger, peeled and finely sliced
3 black cardamom pods (glossary), bruised
coriander (cilantro) sprigs, to garnish

METHOD
Place the rice grains in a mortar and pound into a fine powder. Add the rice wine and mix until well combined.

Place the pork in a large mixing bowl. Add the rice wine mixture, massaging the liquid into the skin. Allow to marinate for at least 30 minutes.

Transfer the pork to a saucepan and cover with cold water. Now add the sugar, ginger, cardamom and a pinch of sea salt. Bring to the boil, then skim off any impurities that rise to the surface.

Cover with a lid, reduce the heat to low and simmer for 3 hours, or until the pork is tender.

Garnish with coriander and serve.

INGREDIENTS

10 cm (4 inch) piece of Chinese cured pork (glossary), or 100 g (3½ oz) jamón, cut into 5 mm (¼ inch) slices
4 garlic cloves, finely sliced
1 green capsicum (pepper), sliced
1 red capsicum (pepper), sliced
200 g (7 oz) fresh ox liver mushrooms or porcini mushrooms, sliced
200 g (7 oz) fresh shiitake mushrooms, sliced
2 young garlic shoots (glossary), cut into 5 cm (2 inch) lengths
2 tablespoons shaoxing rice wine (glossary)

WILD MUSHROOMS WOK-TOSSED WITH CURED PORK
SERVES 4-6 as part of a shared meal

I woke up super-early to attend the bustling Shaxi market, which is only held on Friday mornings. The Bai and Yi people walk for hours from the mountains and valleys, bringing livestock and fresh produce to sell. I was searching for the much-loved ox liver mushroom, which is actually very similar to the great porcini mushroom. These wild mushrooms have ten times more flavour than regular button mushrooms, and their natural glutamate sets off a lovely 'umami' character – the 'fifth taste'.

If you can't obtain either of these mushrooms, an assortment of fresh Asian mushrooms – enoki, shimeji, king brown, oyster, shiitake – is perfect.

METHOD

Heat a wok over high heat, without any oil. Add the pork and cook for 2 minutes, to allow the fat to render.

Add the garlic and capsicums and stir-fry for 1 minute. Now add the mushrooms and garlic shoots and stir-fry for a further 2 minutes.

Add the rice wine and a pinch of sea salt. Stir-fry for another 2 minutes, or until heated through, then serve.

CHINA

Lijiang is a well-preserved city of ethnic minorities, the largest group being the Naxi. High on a plateau, 2400 metres above sea level, Lijiang is bordered by the tree-covered Lion Mountain in the west, Elephant Mountain in the north, and vast fertile fields in the south-east. Crystal-clear streams run through it, making Lijiang one of the most picturesque towns in Yunnan province. With its 800-year history, Lijiang blends ancient tradition with vibrant modern living. Sure, I enjoyed the nightclubs, but what I loved most were the unique Naxi dishes on offer.

Lijiang

While walking through the many narrow cobbled streets of Lijiang, I found a cute Naxi restaurant with a kitchen that opened out onto the footpath. Naturally I stuck my head in, and it was there that I learned of an astonishing dish called '1000 layer pork'. The pork belly was marinated, half cooked, cooled, sliced, carefully layered into a bowl of pickled mustard greens and then steamed for hours, resulting in a dish of incredible flavour and depth.

I couldn't leave Lijiang without learning how to make baba, a crisp, flat bread, and a staple of the Naxi people. I had tried to make it once before, but couldn't get the multiple layering in the dough that makes it truly authentic. Help came in the form of Naxi grandmother Aiyee.

We met at the amazingly beautiful Black Dragon Pool, just outside the old town. It was like looking at a living painting. Up high in the clouds stood Jade Dragon Snow Mountain, reflecting its image onto the spring water below. From here we collected our spring water, as Aiyee said it is very important to make your baba from spring water, not tap water. Back in her village, set among the wheat fields, she taught me how to make sweet baba (page 52).

Just outside the bustling Lijiang markets, I discovered stalls chargrilling what looked like big balls of clay. It was a dish called beggar's chicken, and of course there's a story behind it, which goes like this ... During the Qing dynasty, a starving beggar stole a chicken from a feudal lord. He wanted to cook it, but he was afraid the villagers would smell it being cooked and he would be caught. So he wrapped the chicken in a lotus leaf and smothered it in mud, to keep in the cooking smells. Once it was cooked, he smashed open the mud casing and found that the feathers came right off the chicken, exposing juicy, tender meat that emitted an incredible aroma. The roasted chicken was so delicious that he decided to sell his creation to the villagers. He had unwittingly started one of China's great culinary traditions.

INGREDIENTS

800 g (1 lb 12 oz) whole carp or barramundi, cleaned
generous pinch of chilli flakes, to taste
2 tablespoons peanut oil
1 teaspoon sichuan peppercorns
½ teaspoon sea salt
10 large whole dried red chillies
2 garlic cloves, finely diced
1 young garlic shoot (glossary), finely diced
2 spring onions (scallions), sliced
2 tablespoons roasted crushed unsalted peanuts
250 ml (8½ fl oz/1 cup) vegetable oil
20 mint leaves

CHARGRILLED FISH WITH CRISP MINT

SERVES 4 as part of a shared meal

Lijiang's market was the first building in the entire town, and has been its focal point for hundreds of years. The produce is both amazing and surprising, and the place buzzes with energy. I decided to cook this dish right in the middle of the market – a big mistake! Locals demanded that I first catch my own fish with my bare hands, then kept laughing and pointing while I was grilling the fish. It was nerve-racking, but fun.

METHOD

Heat a chargrill pan or barbecue chargrill to medium–high. Season the fish with a generous pinch of sea salt, freshly ground black pepper and chilli flakes. Rub the fish with 1 tablespoon of the peanut oil, then chargrill on each side for 8–10 minutes.

Meanwhile, dry-roast the sichuan peppercorns and sea salt in a heavy-based frying pan over medium–low heat until the peppercorns become aromatic. Remove from the heat and transfer to a small bowl to cool a little.

Heat the remaining peanut oil in the same pan, then add the dried chillies and cook for 1 minute, or until they become darker all over. Add the diced garlic and garlic shoot and stir-fry over medium–high heat until slightly golden; take care not to let the chillies burn.

Now add the spring onion, peanuts and the dry-roasted sichuan peppercorn and salt mixture. Stir-fry for another 30 seconds, then remove from the heat and set aside.

In a small saucepan, heat the vegetable oil to 170°C (325°F), or until a cube of bread dropped into the oil browns in 20 seconds. Flash-fry the mint leaves in small batches for a few seconds, just until crisp but not browned. Drain well on paper towels.

Once the fish has finished cooking, transfer it to a platter. Spoon the spice and peanut mixture over the top, garnish with the fried mint leaves and serve.

I tried this cold noodle dish on the streets just outside the Black Dragon Pools in Lijiang. I found it very similar to a vermicelli noodle dish from Vietnam, which is probably why I loved it so much. The textures are incredible, and the flavours deep with character.
I now keep garlic water, sichuan pepper oil and yunnan chilli oil in my pantry, so I can whip up this dish in no time!

INGREDIENTS

400 g (14 oz) cooked round Chinese rice noodles, at room temperature
½ Lebanese (short) cucumber, cut into matchsticks
1 small handful bean sprouts
5 garlic chives, cut into 4 cm (1½ inch) lengths
4 coriander (cilantro) stems, roughly chopped
1 spring onion (scallion), finely sliced
1 tablespoon roasted crushed unsalted peanuts

DRESSING

2 teaspoons brown sugar
1 tablespoon Chinese red vinegar (glossary)
1 tablespoon Chinese black vinegar
2 tablespoons light soy sauce
2 teaspoons Garlic Water (see Note, page 33)
2 teaspoons Yunnan Chilli Oil (see page 33)
2 teaspoons Sichuan Pepper Oil (see Note)

LIJIANG COLD NOODLES

SERVES 2

METHOD

Combine the dressing ingredients in a mixing bowl and stir until the sugar has dissolved. Set aside and allow the flavours to infuse for 10 minutes.

Place the noodles in a bowl, along with the rest of the ingredients. Pour the dressing over, toss well and serve.

NOTE

To make sichuan pepper oil, heat 125 ml (4 fl oz/½ cup) peanut oil in a wok until it almost reaches smoking point. Turn off the heat and allow the oil to cool for 3 minutes. Place 2 tablespoons sichuan peppercorns in a glass jar, then pour the hot oil into the jar, followed by 1 tablespoon sesame oil. Allow to cool slightly before sealing; do not strain or discard the peppercorns. The oil will keep for up to a month stored in a cool, dark place.

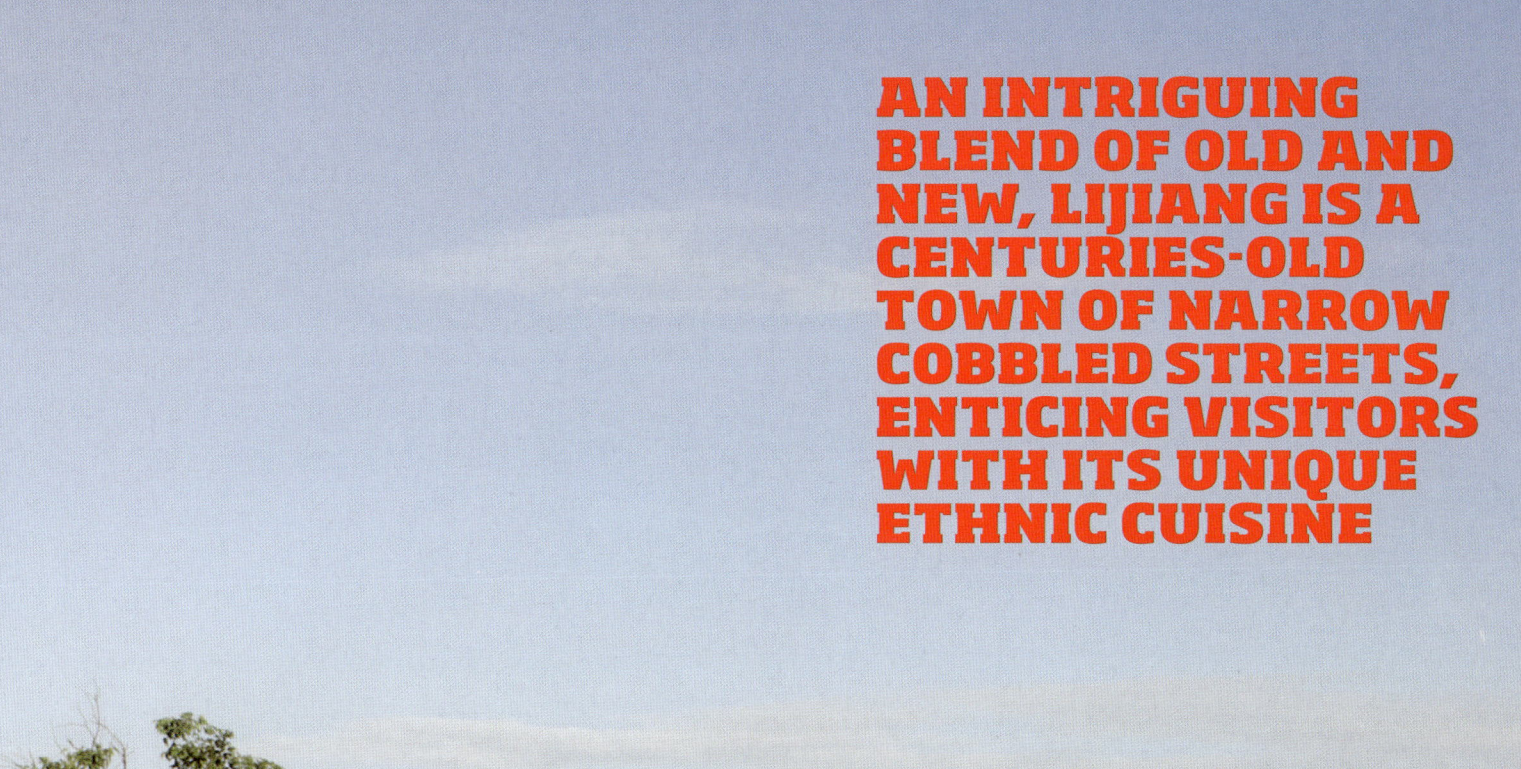

AN INTRIGUING BLEND OF OLD AND NEW, LIJIANG IS A CENTURIES-OLD TOWN OF NARROW COBBLED STREETS, ENTICING VISITORS WITH ITS UNIQUE ETHNIC CUISINE

In the back alleys of Lijiang's old town, I stumbled across a gem of a restaurant serving traditional Naxi cuisine. It had a great kitchen, which opened out onto the streets, so you could see the chefs in action. Wok-burners were roaring, chopping boards were drumming, and steamers were busy slow-cooking this Naxi favourite. Although it doesn't literally have 1000 layers of pork, this dish does look impressive with its many layers of finely sliced pork belly. You can buy pickled mustard greens at your local Asian market in vacuum-sealed bags; choose the Chinese variety, which has a bit of chilli through it. The mustard greens are essential to this dish, cutting through the richness of the pork belly.

INGREDIENTS

500 g (1 lb 2 oz) boneless pork belly, skin scored
250 g (9 oz) pickled mustard greens (glossary)
1 tablespoon vegetable oil
coriander (cilantro) leaves, to garnish, optional
steamed jasmine rice, to serve

MARINADE

2 tablespoons light soy sauce
1 tablespoon dark soy sauce
2 tablespoons shaoxing rice wine (glossary)
3 garlic cloves, finely diced
4 cm (1½ inch) piece of fresh ginger, peeled and finely sliced
2 teaspoons brown sugar

ONE THOUSAND LAYER PORK BELLY

SERVES 4

METHOD

Combine the marinade ingredients in a bowl and stir until the sugar has dissolved. Coat the pork with the marinade, then cover and marinate in the refrigerator for 1 hour.

Meanwhile, soak the pickled mustard greens in cold water for 1 hour, or until very well chilled and firm. Strain well and slice finely. Set aside.

Remove the pork from the marinade, reserving the marinade. Brush off any garlic or ginger pieces from the surface of the pork and pat the pork dry with paper towels.

Heat a deep, heavy-based frying pan over medium heat. Add the vegetable oil, then place the pork skin side down in the pan and brown for 4 minutes. Turn over and brown the other side for a further 4 minutes.

Pour just enough hot water into the pan to cover the pork. Bring to the boil, then reduce the heat and simmer for 10 minutes.

Now submerge the pork belly in an ice bath and leave to cool for 5 minutes – this will make it much easier to slice it finely. (Alternatively, you can cool it, then cover and place in the freezer for 1 hour.)

Slice the pork as finely as you can, using a large sharp knife. Arrange each slice in a heatproof bowl, overlapping the slices neatly, with the fat end on top, creating a '1000 layer' effect across the bowl and up the edges.

Arrange the mustard greens on top of the layered pork, then pour in the reserved marinade.

Half-fill a steamer, wok or large saucepan with water and bring to a rapid boil over high heat. Place the bowl of pork in a steamer basket, then set over the pan of boiling water and cover. Steam for 1½ hours, replenishing the hot water as needed every 30 minutes or so.

Remove the bowl from the steamer. Place a serving plate upside down over the bowl, then angle it until the liquid from the pork pours out, catching the liquid in a bowl. Allow the pork to cool for 10 minutes.

With the plate still on top of the bowl, quickly invert the bowl, so that the bowl is now on top of the serving plate. Remove the bowl and pour the liquid over the pork.

Garnish with coriander, if desired, and serve with steamed jasmine rice.

INGREDIENTS

300 g (10½ oz/2 cups) plain (all-purpose) flour
½ teaspoon bicarbonate of soda (baking soda)
200 ml (7 fl oz) sparkling spring water
40 g (1½ oz/¼ cup) unsalted roasted peanuts
25 g (1 oz/¼ cup) roasted walnuts
2 teaspoons black sesame seeds
1 tablespoon caster (superfine) sugar
1 tablespoon brown sugar
250 g (9 oz/1 cup) lard

TRADITIONAL NAXI SWEET BABA

MAKES 24 pieces (SERVES 4–6)

Ancient traders took this crisp, flaky flat bread on their long trips along the 'Tea Horse Trail', as it travelled well and sustained them. A staple in the Naxi diet, baba is eaten with everything. Some are plain; others stuffed with spring onions (scallions), pork or eggs; I've even tried baba smeared with preserved bean curd. While they were all delicious, this sweet version, taught to me by a local lady named Aiyee, is the one I enjoyed most. Aiyee says it is essential to follow her folding tips, to create the much-needed multi-layered texture of this sweet baba. It is also important to use lard in this recipe, as it makes the pastry light and flaky.

METHOD

Combine the flour, bicarbonate of soda and water in a bowl and mix until a coarse dough forms. Knead on a lightly floured work surface to a smooth dough, repeatedly folding the dough back onto itself as you knead, to incorporate air into it. The folding technique is essential for a baba – you need to 'fold' the dough as you knead it, to get enough air through it. Cover the dough with a tea towel (dish towel) and leave to rest for 10 minutes.

Meanwhile, using a large mortar and pestle, pound the peanuts, walnuts and sesame seeds together into a fine powder. Add the sugars and mix well.

Divide the rested dough into three evenly sized balls. Using a rolling pin, roll each portion out to an oval about 30 cm (12 inches) long, 12 cm (4¾ inches) wide and 5 mm (¼ inch) thick. Now spread 1 tablespoon of the lard on top of each oval.

Starting from the bottom of each oval, and working with one piece at a time, tightly roll up the dough, creating nice firm rolls about 15 cm (6 inches) wide.

Working with one piece at a time, hold the roll at each end, then twist the roll tightly in opposite directions, to form a tight, twisted rope. This helps create more layers in the dough. Fold the twisted roll in half lengthways, then use the palms of your hands to flatten the whole thing. Holding one end down, use your other hand to further knead and work the dough out until it is 1 cm (½ inch) thick and perfectly round.

Using both hands, and again working with one round at a time, cup each round in your hand and work it with your thumb to form a deep cup shape in your palm. Now form a pocket in the dough portions, deep enough to spoon in a generous tablespoon of the nut mixture. Enclose the pocket by pinching the edges with your fingers until it looks like a round bun.

Now use the rolling pin to roll each bun into a perfect round shape, 1 cm (½ inch) thick.

Heat a frying pan over medium heat and add one third of the remaining lard. Fry one baba for 2–3 minutes on each side, or until golden brown and crisp. Repeat with the other two baba rounds.

Slice each baba into eight pieces, as you would a pizza, and serve.

CHINA

Xishuangbanna is in the southernmost reaches of China, bordering Laos and Myanmar. Like its neighbours in the greater Mekong region, it has a subtropical climate. Nicknamed the Kingdom of the Plants, it is formally known as 'Sipsongpanna', which sounds more Thai than Chinese, and means 'twelve thousand rice fields'.

It was here I began to get a taste of South-East Asia and saw the start of the mighty Mekong, which helped me understand China's important role in preserving the great river. How China treats the river affects six other countries, and 60 million people who depend on it for their daily survival.

Xishuangbanna

Xishuangbanna is also the most important tea-growing region in China, and home to the famous and much-loved Pu-erh tea, which spawned a complex series of trading routes criss-crossing China, Tibet, Nepal, Myanmar and India over some of the world's highest terrain. These routes were collectively known as the Tea Horse Trail.

The best Pu-erh tea comes from an area called 'Six Famous Mountains', a place of breathtaking beauty. Steeply terraced tea plantations stretch as far as the eye can see, worked by local ladies wearing colourful garb and bamboo baskets on their backs. Their bright, contagious smiles had me diving in to help with the picking.

Six Famous Mountains has been a tea-growing region for more than 2000 years, and the ladies told me that tea wasn't only used for drinking – tea leaves have also been used in medicine, and as money. We discussed different food dishes that tea leaves are used in, mainly for their fragrance. I immediately thought of a sweet snack my grandmother used to make when I was a kid – sticky sesame-coated rice balls, filled with caramelised sugar cane and cooked in a tea broth. I just had to cook it for the ladies.

I put my tea broth on the boil, but suddenly torrential rain began bucketing down. Our small umbrellas were no match for the elements and within seconds my dumpling dough was drowned in rainwater, and my back-up rice flour was absolutely soaked. We took cover in a grass hut among the tea fields, huddling together to keep warm until the rain stopped. Then we tried again. Looking back, it was hilarious and lots of fun.

When I arrived in Xishuangbanna, I was surprised at how much it resembles Thailand. It was hot, humid and tropical, and I noticed lemongrass was abundant in this area. Throughout the markets, street-food stalls would be chargrilling this aromatic fish dish, which got me hooked and made me curious to try it out for myself.

It may be difficult to find the upper green long leaves of the lemongrass to tie the fish with, if you don't actually grow it yourself in the garden. If so, just peel each outer layer of the lemongrass stem until you have enough to cover the chargrill, then cook your fish on top of that.

INGREDIENTS

2 whole lemongrass stems
1 spring onion (scallion), finely sliced
1 garlic clove, finely chopped
½ long red chilli, finely sliced
2.5 cm (1 inch) piece of fresh ginger, peeled and finely chopped
1 tablespoon light soy sauce
600 g (1 lb 5 oz) whole tilapia or snapper, cleaned
1 tablespoon vegetable oil

CHARGRILLED LEMONGRASS TILAPIA

SERVES 4 as part of a shared meal

METHOD

Cut off the long green stems of the lemongrass, then cut down along the stems to separate the leaves. Soak the leaves in a large bowl of warm water for 20 minutes to soften them a little.

Meanwhile, finely dice the white ends of the lemongrass, then place in a mixing bowl with the spring onion, garlic, chilli, ginger and soy sauce. Mix well and set aside.

Lay the fish on a chopping board. Using a sharp filleting knife, start from the head end of the fish and create a fillet by slicing down from the spine to the belly, but don't cut the fillet off the body – just leave it lying open, and still attached to the bone along the belly.

Now spread the lemongrass mixture over the exposed part of the fillet, then close the fish back up. Tie the reserved lemongrass stems around the fish to keep it closed, or secure the opening with toothpicks.

Heat a barbecue chargrill or chargrill pan to medium-high. Brush the fish with the vegetable oil, then chargrill for 10 minutes on each side, or until the flesh flakes easily when tested with a fork. Cut away the lemongrass leaves and serve.

CHICKEN & HERBS WRAPPED IN BANANA LEAF

SERVES 4 as part of a shared meal

INGREDIENTS

300 g (10½ oz) boneless, skinless chicken thighs, minced (ground)
2 garlic cloves, finely chopped
4 cm (1½ inch) piece of fresh ginger, peeled and finely sliced
2 tablespoons soy sauce
4 fresh or frozen acacia herb (cha-om) stems (glossary), roughly chopped
10 Thai basil leaves
1 lemongrass stem, white part only, finely chopped
2 spring onions (scallions), sliced
3 small whole red chillies
3 small whole green chillies
5 fresh betel leaves (glossary), finely sliced
5 saw-tooth coriander (cilantro) leaves (glossary), sliced
1 tablespoon vegetable oil
pinch of cornflour (cornstarch)
2 banana leaves, each about 60 cm (24 inches) long, central rib removed
Sticky Rice (page 166), to serve

METHOD

Combine all the ingredients, except the banana leaves and sticky rice, in a large mixing bowl. Add a generous pinch of sea salt and freshly ground black pepper. Mix well, then allow the flavours to infuse for 15 minutes.

Meanwhile, heat a barbecue chargrill or chargrill pan to medium-high. Place the banana leaves on the chargrill for a minute on each side, to soften them and make them easier to work with.

Now place one leaf, shiny side down, vertically on your work surface. Place the other leaf, shiny side down, horizontally across the middle of the first leaf to form a cross.

Now place the chicken mixture in the middle of the leaves. Flatten the filling out to form a 20 cm (8 inch) square. Fold the leaves up, one side at a time, over the filling, to form one big secure parcel.

Place the parcel on the chargrill, seam side down. Cook for 15 minutes on each side.

Cut the leaves open and serve the mixture with sticky rice.

Originally from Thailand and Laos, the Dai ethnic minority settled along the banks of the Mekong in Xishuangbanna. Walking through their village I noticed shiny golden temples, monks in orange robes and tall wooden stilt homes, just like in Thailand. So it was no surprise the local food had a strong Thai influence.

If you can't find fresh acacia herb (cha-om), you can buy it frozen at your local Thai market. Don't be put off by its pungent smell: once cooked, it is aromatic, and adds so much depth.

This dish is perfect when you're feeling a little under the weather, as the mixed fresh herbs have great medicinal qualities.

Tea formed the basis of an important and complex series of trading routes that criss-crossed south-west China, connecting the country to Tibet, Nepal, Myanmar and India. Crossing some of the highest terrain in the world, these routes were collectively known as the 'Tea Horse Trail'. Green tea imparts a great fragrance to these sweet, sticky, chewy dumplings. As I was making them among the tea fields, it began bucketing with rain, so I thought I might as well collect the rainwater for my dumpling skins. They turned out perfect.

INGREDIENTS

75 g (2½ oz) glutinous rice flour
35 g (1¼ oz) rice flour
¼ teaspoon salt
20 g (¾ oz) dark palm sugar (jaggery), chopped into small pieces
2 tablespoons green tea leaves
½ teaspoon white sesame seeds, toasted
½ teaspoon black sesame seeds, toasted

TEA-INFUSED STICKY SESAME DUMPLINGS
MAKES 12

METHOD

In a mixing bowl, combine the rice flours and the salt. Add 100 ml (3½ fl oz) water and stir with a spoon until the mixture is well combined and comes together as a sticky but smooth dough.

Divide the dough into 12 equal portions. Roll each portion into a small ball.

Working with one portion at a time, push on each one with your thumb to form a small hollow in the centre. Place ½ teaspoon of the palm sugar in each one. Seal the hollow by squeezing the dough together over it, then gently roll each dumpling into a neat ball shape again, pinching to seal well. Place on plastic wrap so they don't stick to the work surface.

Bring a large saucepan of water to the boil and add the tea leaves. Working in two batches, boil the dumplings for 6 minutes, or until they rise to the surface.

Remove with a slotted spoon, allowing the water to drain off, and place the dumplings straight onto a serving platter.

Sprinkle with the sesame seeds and serve hot.

CHINA – XISHUANGBANNA

TAKING A BREAK ALONG THE TEA HORSE TRAIL, WITH LOCAL LADIES IN COLOURFUL ATTIRE

CHAPTER 2

Myanmar
YANGON TO KENGTUNG

Myanmar
YANGON TO KENGTUNG

Myanmar is Asia's hidden gem. Most people still know it as Burma, but it has been more than 20 years since the country's name changed. Despite the political attention this nation has received, nothing prepared me for what I found.

To call it a secret paradise would probably be too much, but the respect these generous people have for each other, their sense of community and their moral standards moved me to tears on more than one occasion. In many ways, life in Myanmar is what I imagine life was like a long time ago.

When I first told people I was going to Myanmar, and would be looking specifically at its regional foods, I was surprised at how many of them warned me against it. They said the food was terrible, that it all tasted the same – a bit like Indian food but less interesting.

I was astounded that the food of a country nestled between China, Thailand, India, Bangladesh and Laos would not have been influenced by its neighbours, or have developed its own exciting cuisine. My apprehension disappeared the first time I tried the national dish, mohinga.

Mohinga is a delicious soup of great texture and flavour, suited to any time of the day. It was just the first of so many dishes that I was offered and came to love.

We were amazed by the generous nature of the local people. Everyone I spoke to wanted the international community to recognise them, to visit and bring new opportunities to the country. The group I travelled with were the very first international television crew to visit Myanmar with permission to film and document the people's lives, based on their food and traditions.

Myanmar is best known for its political unrest and its international boycotts, but I was not there to look at these things; I was there to experience the people, the landscape, the food and, to my surprise, some really good local wine!

Based on all these things, Myanmar is one of my favourite South-East Asian countries.

I started my trip in the former capital Yangon, where I explored the almost endless streets filled with busy markets and roadside vendors, before heading into the Shan state, where I discovered my favourite Shan dish, 'tofu nwe', on the shores of Inle Lake. Next, I travelled northeast, stopping at Kengtung, a quiet, picturesque town surrounded by rustic hill tribe villages and ancient Buddhist monasteries.

Never have I visited a country where the locals were so warm and inviting. People would say, again and again, "You are my guest, please, we are so honoured to have you. Take the heart of Myanmar to the world, and let them come to visit us."

YANGON IS A RICHLY LAYERED HOTPOT OF MYANMAR, BRITISH, CHINESE AND INDIAN INFLUENCES, BUT ITS REAL SPIRIT IS IN THE STREETS, FILLED WITH FOOD MARKETS AND VENDORS OF EVERY KIND

MYANMAR

Visiting Yangon, the former capital of Myanmar, is an experience like no other. Before independence in 1948, the country was considered a province of British India. The city is a combination of British, Myanmar, Chinese and Indian influences, and is known for its colonial architecture. Yangon is home to the Shwedagon Pagoda, built 2500 years ago to enshrine eight strands of Buddha's hair. It remains an important pilgrimage site for the Myanmar people, and for Buddhists from around the world. The spirit of Yangon is undeniably in its colourful, lively streets, filled with markets, street food and vendors of every kind.

Whenever I visit a new country, my first point of call, to discover the cuisine and culture, is always the local markets. In my first three minutes in Yangon I learnt three new things: banana trunks are used in cooking; sandalwood is used to protect the skin from the sun; and Myanmar's national dish is mohinga. I tried mohinga for the first time and fell in love with it immediately. Its flavour and texture was far too complex for me to be able to pinpoint every ingredient, so I grabbed my banana trunk and set off to meet Kin-Kin, a mohinga specialist.

I connected instantly with Kin-Kin – it was like hanging out with my great-auntie. We talked of food, ingredients, flavours, aromas, cooking techniques, traditions and her love for Myanmar. I'll never forget her words as she spooned the bright yellow turmeric powder into the sizzling pan: 'Myanmar is the Golden Land'.

With the intricacies of the national dish under my belt, I made my way to Shwedagon, a spectacular illuminated golden pagoda standing on a hill overlooking the city. Local legend says it was built during the time of the Buddha. As I entered its sacred grounds, I instantly felt its spiritual energy. People come from all over the country to worship, with many donating money or gold to the temple. Its tip is encrusted with over 7000 diamonds and rubies, and it was built from more than 21,000 solid gold bars.

What I love about Yangon is that in the centre of town there is a Buddhist temple, sitting across the road from a Catholic church, which is next door to a Muslim mosque – all living and worshipping in harmony. A city of so many different cultures and beliefs means there are also many food styles. I found a family making Chinese egg noodles, a street stall grilling roti, a tea shop pouring black tea with condensed milk, a factory making popiah skins (page 75) and busy eateries serving spicy curries.

Rarely are film crews granted access into this intriguing city. We felt we were definitely discovering the unknown.

INGREDIENTS

4 Japanese eggplants (aubergines)
2 red Asian shallots, finely sliced
1 handful coriander (cilantro), torn
1 tablespoon Garlic Oil (see Note, page 82)
1 tablespoon light soy sauce
juice of ½ lime
1 teaspoon sesame seeds, toasted
1 teaspoon Fried Garlic (see Note, page 82)
1 teaspoon Fried Red Asian Shallots (see Note, page 155)
6 cooked tiger prawns (shrimp), peeled and deveined
2 teaspoons roasted crushed unsalted peanuts

CHARGRILLED EGGPLANT & PRAWN SALAD

SERVES 4 as part of a shared meal

The kingly eggplant is actually a fruit – part of the nightshade family, along with tomatoes, potatoes, capsicum (peppers) and tobacco.

Here I use Japanese eggplants as they are skinny, long and have thin skin, making them perfect for chargrilling. The cooked flesh becomes moist and creamy and takes on a lovely deep smokiness, which is my favourite character of this dish.

When I cooked this recipe on the streets of Yangon, all the local food-stall owners offered to give up their chargrill barbecue for me. I couldn't accept, as it meant they couldn't operate their own stall. But they were adamant on helping, so off they went and brought back their family barbecue from home! The people of Myanmar would have to be among the most generous in the world.

METHOD

Pierce each eggplant several times using a sharp knife, to prevent them bursting on the grill. Heat a barbecue chargrill or chargrill pan to medium.

Chargrill the eggplants for 10 minutes, or until charred all over and soft to touch, turning often.

Place the eggplants under cold slow running water and peel off and discard the charred skin.

Now slice the eggplants into 2 cm (¾ inch) pieces and place in a mixing bowl. Add the remaining ingredients, reserving half the peanuts as a garnish. Add a pinch of sea salt and freshly ground black pepper and combine well.

Transfer to a serving bowl and arrange a few of the prawns on top. Sprinkle with the remaining peanuts and serve.

INGREDIENTS

1 tablespoon peanut oil
1 garlic clove, finely chopped
75 g (2½ oz) bean sprouts
65 g (2¼ oz/½ cup) grated daikon radish
1 small carrot, grated
50 g (2 oz) young fresh or tinned bamboo shoots, finely sliced
75 g (2½ oz/1 cup) finely shredded Chinese cabbage
25 g (¾ oz) glass noodles, soaked in hot water for 20 minutes, then drained
60 g (2 oz/½ cup) finely sliced Asian celery (glossary)
1 small spring onion (scallion), finely sliced
50 g (2 oz) fried tofu puffs, finely sliced
¼ teaspoon sea salt
¼ teaspoon sugar
1 tablespoon light soy sauce
12 butter lettuce leaves
12 popiah skins (see recipe below, or use frozen ones)
1½ tablespoons Fried Garlic (see Note, page 82)
1½ tablespoons Fried Red Asian Shallots (see Note, page 155)
1½ tablespoons chopped peanuts
Chinese-style chilli sauce, for dipping

POPIAH SKINS

500 g (1 lb 2 oz) plain (all-purpose) flour
2 teaspoons sea salt

VEGETABLE SPRING ROLLS

MAKES 12 (SERVES 4)

METHOD

To make the popiah skins, use an electric mixer with a paddle attachment to beat the flour, salt and 500 ml (17 fl oz/2 cups) water on medium-high speed for 30 minutes. The dough will be ready when it is smooth, rubbery and comes away from the side of the bowl. Now knead the dough by hand, by repeatedly lifting it up and slamming it back down into the bowl until it starts to hold together in ropes. Cover and refrigerate for at least 30 minutes.

Meanwhile, heat a wok over medium-high heat. Add the peanut oil and sauté the garlic for 1 minute, or until fragrant. Add the bean sprouts, daikon, carrot, bamboo shoots, cabbage and noodles and stir-fry for 2 minutes. Now add the celery, spring onion and tofu and stir-fry for a further minute. Season with the salt, sugar and soy sauce and stir-fry for 1 minute more. Remove the mixture from the wok and leave to cool for 5 minutes.

Divide the dough into about five small batches for easy handling. Heat a 26 cm (10½ inch) non-stick crepe pan over medium heat. Hold the dough with one hand and smear it over the hot pan in a circular motion, only just covering the surface of the pan. The dough should be extremely thin, and barely but evenly covering the base of the pan. Cook for 1 minute, or until the edge of the crepe starts to curl up. Using your other hand, carefully peel the skin from the pan and place it on a plate. Continue making more skins until the dough is finished. (Any unused sheets can be frozen.)

To assemble the rolls, place a lettuce leaf on a popiah skin, then place a little vegetable mixture lengthways over the lettuce. Add a sprinkle of fried garlic, fried shallots and peanuts. Roll the bottom up, then fold the left and right sides in, creating an envelope. Now keep rolling up, into a nice tight roll. Repeat with the remaining ingredients.

Slice each roll into thirds and serve with chilli sauce.

Walking down 17th Street in Yangon I stumbled across a kitchen with six sweaty young cooks making popiah skins from rice flour and water. Popiah ('kaw pyant') means 'thin crepe'. Originating in China, this dish made its way through Malaysia and Singapore to Myanmar. It was incredible to watch the grace and skill of those cooks; they made it look so easy. When I gave it a go I ended up splattered with batter! If making the popiah skins at home, try to get hold of a thin, non-stick crepe pan, to make the crepes as thin as possible.

INGREDIENTS

8 raw jumbo king prawns (shrimp), peeled and deveined, leaving the head and tail intact
large pinch of ground turmeric
large pinch of sea salt
1 tablespoon fish sauce
4 ripe tomatoes, sliced
1 teaspoon sugar
½ teaspoon sweet paprika
coriander (cilantro) leaves, to garnish

SPICE PASTE

5 red Asian shallots, roughly chopped
3 garlic cloves, peeled
4 cm (1½ inch) piece of fresh galangal, peeled and sliced
3 dried chillies, soaked in hot water for 10 minutes, then drained
60 ml (2 fl oz/¼ cup) peanut oil
2 teaspoons ground turmeric

KING PRAWN & TOMATO CURRY
SERVES 4

Myanmar cuisine has a strong Indian influence, evident in the varieties of amazing curries on offer. However the Myanmar curry has developed its own identity; it is not as spicy, heavy or rich as a typical Indian curry. This dish is a perfect example of the lighter and more delicate Myanmar style of curry. When cooking your curry paste, make sure you give it time to slowly caramelise. In Myanmar this process is called 'sipyan', meaning to 'allow the oils to return'. This process is essential in Myanmar cooking.

METHOD

Coat the prawns with the turmeric, salt and 2 teaspoons of the fish sauce. Leave to marinate for 10 minutes.

To make the spice paste, pound the shallot, garlic, galangal and chillies into a fine paste using a large mortar and pestle, or in a food processor.

Heat the peanut oil in a wok or saucepan over very low heat. Add the spice paste and turmeric and sauté for 15 minutes, or until slightly caramelised.

Stir in the tomatoes, sugar, paprika, remaining fish sauce and 125 ml (4 fl oz/½ cup) water. Simmer for 10 minutes, or until the sauce is thick and the tomatoes have broken down.

Add the prawns and cook for 2 minutes on each side. Garnish with coriander and serve.

INGREDIENTS

100 g (3½ oz) rice vermicelli noodles
2 hard-boiled eggs, halved
100 g (3½ oz) boiled banana trunk heart (glossary), sliced, optional
4 coriander (cilantro) sprigs, to garnish
4 snake (yard-long) beans, finely sliced
chilli flakes, for sprinkling
lime wedges, to serve

BROTH

1 kg (2 lb 3 oz) whole catfish or silver perch, cleaned
1 lemongrass stem, bruised
2 garlic cloves, bashed
1 teaspoon ground turmeric
3 tablespoons tinned chickpeas, mashed
85 g (3 oz/⅓ cup) Toasted Rice Powder (see Note, page 187)
8 red Asian shallots, peeled
80 ml (2½ fl oz/⅓ cup) fish sauce

SPICE PASTE

3 lemongrass stems, white part only, finely sliced
4 whole dried chillies, soaked in boiling water for 10 minutes, then drained
4 red Asian shallots, diced
4 garlic cloves, diced
2 cm (¾ inch) piece of fresh ginger, peeled and finely sliced
125 ml (4 fl oz/½ cup) peanut oil
2 teaspoons shrimp paste
1 teaspoon ground turmeric
1 teaspoon sweet paprika

MOHINGA

SERVES 4

METHOD

To make the broth, place the whole fish in a large saucepan with the lemongrass, garlic and turmeric. Add enough cold water to cover the fish and bring to the boil. Skim off any impurities, then reduce the heat to low and simmer for 20 minutes. Strain the broth and reserve it. Remove the fish meat from the bones, discarding the skin and bones.

Meanwhile, make a start on your spice paste. Pound the lemongrass, whole dried chillies, shallot, garlic and ginger into a smooth paste using a large mortar and pestle, or in a food processor.

Heat the peanut oil in a saucepan over low heat. Add the spice mixture and sauté for 20 minutes, or until slightly caramelised. Stir in the shrimp paste, turmeric and paprika. Now add the flaked fish, mixing gently until the fish is well coated. Cook over low heat for a further 5 minutes, to allow the flavours to infuse.

Return the broth to the large saucepan. Add the fish mixture, mashed chickpeas, rice powder, shallots, fish sauce and a pinch of sea salt and freshly ground black pepper. Stir to combine, then simmer for 30 minutes.

Meanwhile, cook the noodles in a saucepan of boiling water for 2 minutes, then remove the pan from the heat and stand the noodles in the water for 5 minutes. Drain well, rinse under cold water, then drain well again.

Add the boiled eggs to the broth, with the banana trunk, if using.

Divide the noodles among four bowls, then ladle the broth over the noodles. Garnish with the coriander, snake beans and chilli flakes and serve with lime wedges.

'Mohinga' translates as a 'soup snack'. This noodle soup is Myanmar's beloved national dish. It is served on the streets, in the markets, and even in fine restaurants. The Myanmar adore it as much as the Japanese love ramen and the Vietnamese love pho. This intricate, complex dish has many layers of flavours and textures, so it needs some time to create, but it is definitely worth it. Now I do understand it may be difficult to get banana trunk heart from your local Asian store, so you can use finely sliced raw or tinned banana blossom instead – there is no need to boil it before using.

MYANMAR

Inle Lake – a long, hot dusty bus trip north-east of Yangon – is in Myanmar's largest state, called Shan. Nine major ethnic groups call this region home, including the Shan tribe, the second largest in the country. The people here have long been known for their political and cultural independence.
The lake itself is huge, covering about 160 square kilometres, but it wasn't until a boat trip on the lake that I really started to appreciate the area's natural beauty.

Inle Lake

For the Shan people, the lake is their home. Canals are their roads, canoes are their transport, and their backyards are floating gardens. This watery environment literally shapes their village lifestyles.

Most of the people on Inle Lake grow tomatoes – about 61,000 tonnes every year. They don't only pick red tomatoes; locals love using the green ones raw in a salad with chilli, coriander (cilantro) and black sesame seeds. Their green tomatoes are crisp, slightly tart and yet also sweet. Afterwards, back in Sydney, I made the salad with green heirloom tomatoes and everyone loved it.

The other Shan dish that wowed me was 'tofu' noodles. I heard of this unusual regional specialty back in Yangon, and was told I had to try it during my visit. Misuu Borit, owner of the Inle Princess Resort, kindly invited us to her family home to cook this much-loved dish with her mother.

When my boat arrived at her floating stilt home, I was greeted by the whole extended family. There were great-aunties, uncles, cousins, nephews, nieces, grandchildren, in-laws, and even the head chef from the resort, Nwe-Oo. She showed me a huge bucket of chickpeas soaking in water. "This is what we make the tofu from," she said. "Chickpeas – not soya beans."

After we strained the chickpeas, I sat on the timber floor with four family members grinding the softened chickpeas in old stone mills. We then tied thick rope to the beams on the roof, suspended a large wooden frame and tied muslin (cheesecloth) to it, making an enormous strainer to drain the chickpea liquid. We cooked the liquid on low heat until it thickened, then added turmeric, chicken, bok choy (pak choy), rice noodles and bean sprouts and finished it with a lovely sugar cane syrup. The 'tofu' had a texture like custard, and when combined with the silky rice noodles it was unlike any other noodle dish I had ever tried.

Inle Lake is such a special place. The people are among the friendliest in the world. It is a place where I made many lovely friends, and one I will return to soon …

INGREDIENTS

5 green tomatoes, sliced
3 red Asian shallots, sliced
1 handful sliced coriander (cilantro)
2 teaspoons roasted crushed unsalted peanuts
2 teaspoons ground black sesame seeds
½ teaspoon chilli flakes
3 teaspoons Garlic Oil (see Note)

TO GARNISH

1 red chilli, sliced
coriander (cilantro) sprigs
½ teaspoon Fried Garlic (see Note)

INLE LAKE GREEN TOMATO SALAD

SERVES 4 as part of a shared meal

Inle Lake's main sources of income are fishing and growing tomatoes. It was incredible to see how locals actually grow these tomatoes; they are all grown on water, lined up in rows, just like winemakers grow their grape vines. Covering about 7000 acres, these floating farms produce some 61,000 tonnes of tomatoes each year!

I'm using green tomatoes in this salad as I love their crunchy texture and mild, sweet, tangy flavour. Don't go for young green tomatoes; choose mature green ones.

METHOD

In a bowl, combine the tomato, shallot, coriander, peanuts, sesame seeds, chilli flakes, garlic oil and a pinch of sea salt. Mix well.

Garnish with the chilli and coriander, sprinkle with the fried garlic and serve immediately.

NOTE

To make fried garlic and garlic oil, pour 250 ml (9 fl oz/1 cup) vegetable oil into a wok and heat to 180°C (350°F), or until a cube of bread dropped into the oil browns in 15 seconds. Add 6 finely chopped garlic cloves and fry until golden – be careful not to overcook the garlic, as it will keep cooking once it is removed from the heat. Strain the garlic through a metal sieve and place on paper towels to dry. Store the fried garlic in an airtight container for up to 4 days; this recipe makes about 2 tablespoons. Reserve the garlic-flavoured oil to use in salads; it will keep for up to 2 weeks if stored in a cool place.

INGREDIENTS

500 ml (17 fl oz/2 cups) peanut oil, for deep-frying
10 lotus flowers or fresh betel leaves (glossary)

TAMARIND DIPPING SAUCE

125 ml (4 fl oz/½ cup) Tamarind Water (see Note)
2 teaspoons sugar
2 teaspoons fish sauce
2 cm (¾ inch) piece of fresh ginger, peeled and pounded
2 small garlic cloves, peeled and pounded
½ teaspoon chilli flakes
2 tablespoons chopped coriander (cilantro)

FRITTERS

10 spring onions (scallions)
1 ripe tomato, sliced
1 red Asian shallot, finely sliced
2 cm (¾ inch) piece of fresh ginger, peeled and pounded
2 garlic cloves, peeled and pounded
1 teaspoon hot paprika
1 teaspoon sea salt
90 g (3 oz/½ cup) rice flour
45 g (1½ oz/¼ cup) glutinous rice flour
½ teaspoon baking powder
125 ml (4 fl oz/½ cup) beer

This is the tastiest Shan snack, my absolute favourite. It is the perfect drinking dish – or as the ladies in Myanmar call it, a 'gossiping' dish. The filling may feel a little moist and loose, but it will all come together and crisp up as you deep-fry it. Traditionally, these fritters are wrapped up in pretty lotus flowers and dipped in the tamarind sauce, but betel leaves work well too.

CRISP SPRING ONION FRITTERS

MAKES 10

METHOD

Put the dipping sauce ingredients in a bowl and mix until well combined. Set aside until ready to serve.

To make the fritters, cut the green parts of the spring onion into 3 cm (1¼ inch) lengths and finely slice the white ends. Place in a bowl with the tomato, shallot, ginger, garlic, paprika and salt. Add the rice flours and baking powder and mix to combine. Slowly stir in the beer, adding just enough so that everything sticks together.

Heat the peanut oil in a wok over high heat; you can tell the oil is hot enough when you drop in a breadcrumb and it starts to cook.

Divide the fritter mixture into 10 even portions, clumping each together to form a fritter about 5-6 cm (2-2¼ inches) across. Add them to the hot oil, in batches if necessary, and fry for 2-3 minutes on each side, or until golden brown and crisp. Drain briefly on paper towels.

Wrap the fritters with a lotus flower or betel leaf and serve with the dipping sauce. Enjoy with beer.

NOTE

To make tamarind water, soak 100 g (3½ oz) tamarind pulp in 400 ml (13 fl oz) boiling water. Break it up a little with a whisk, then leave until cool enough to handle. Using your hands, break the mixture into a thick paste. Pass the mixture through a sieve; you should get about 375 ml (12½ fl oz/1½ cups) tamarind water.

INLE STUFFED FISH

SERVES 4 as part of a shared meal

INGREDIENTS

4 cm (1½ inch) piece of fresh ginger, peeled and chopped
3 garlic cloves, chopped
500 g (1 lb 2 oz) whole carp or barramundi, cleaned
1 teaspoon light soy sauce
½ teaspoon sea salt
60 ml (2 fl oz/¼ cup) peanut oil
125 ml (4 fl oz/½ cup) tomato passata (puréed tomatoes)
¼ teaspoon ground turmeric
1 teaspoon sweet paprika
2 spring onions (scallions), sliced
1 large tomato, diced
vegetable oil, for deep-frying
2 coriander (cilantro) sprigs

METHOD

Using a mortar and pestle, pound the ginger and garlic to a paste, then set aside.

Lay the fish flat on a chopping board. Using a sharp knife, and starting from its spine, carefully slice down towards its belly, on one side only, following the bone line – but don't slice all the way through. This is to create a pocket for the stuffing, about 15 cm (6 inches) long.

Now coat the fish with the soy sauce, salt, and half the ginger and garlic paste. Leave to marinate for 10 minutes.

Heat the peanut oil in a hot pan. Stir in the passata and the remaining garlic and ginger paste. Cook, stirring, over medium heat for 10 minutes. Add the turmeric, paprika and spring onion and cook for a further 5 minutes.

Allow the passata mixture to cool a little, then stuff half the mixture into the pocket in the fish. Secure the pocket by tying the fish back together with kitchen string.

Stir the tomato and 125 ml (4 fl oz/½ cup) hot water into the remaining stuffing mixture and simmer for a further 5 minutes.

Meanwhile, half-fill a wok with vegetable oil and heat to 180°C (350°F), or until a cube of bread dropped into the oil browns in 15 seconds. Add the fish and deep-fry for 8 minutes, or until crisp, turning the fish over halfway during cooking.

Transfer the fish to a serving plate, then cut away and discard the string. Top the fish with the remaining stuffing mixture. Garnish with the coriander and serve.

I was introduced to this dish by a chef from the Karen ethnic minority group, or 'Long Neck' people. Nwe-Oo was so proud of her cuisine and passionate about sharing the beauty of Shan cooking.
I spent many days in her kitchen at Inle Princess Resort, learning the secrets of traditional Myanmar cooking. If only the whole world were as kind-hearted and generous as the people of Myanmar.

FOR THE SHAN PEOPLE, INLE LAKE IS THEIR HOME. CANALS ARE THEIR ROADS, CANOES ARE THEIR TRANSPORT, THEIR BACKYARDS ARE FLOATING GARDENS

SHAN WARM CHICKPEA 'TOFU' NOODLE SOUP

SERVES 4

This most-loved dish in Shan is made from 'tofu', but not your usual soya bean tofu. The 'tofu' is actually made from chickpeas! I was introduced to this dish by a lovely lady named Misuu. I sat with her family grinding soaked chickpeas in a traditional old stone mill – an experience I will never forget. You'll find chickpea flour in health food shops. For this recipe you will need to let it settle in cold water overnight, so start a day ahead.

INGREDIENTS

400 g (14 oz/3⅔ cups) besan (chickpea flour)
60 ml (2 fl oz/⅓ cup) peanut oil
¼ teaspoon ground turmeric
5 red Asian shallots, diced
3 garlic cloves, peeled and pounded
4 cm (1½ inch) piece of fresh ginger, peeled and pounded
3 tomatoes, diced
1 teaspoon sweet paprika
3 boneless, skinless chicken thighs (about 450 g/1 lb), cut into 3 cm (1¼ inch) chunks

TO SERVE

400 g (14 oz) fresh rice noodles, cooked according to packet instructions
200 g (7 oz) baby bok choy (pak choy), leaves separated
200 g (7 oz) bean sprouts
1 tablespoon black sesame seeds
1 tablespoon roasted crushed unsalted peanuts
2 teaspoons Fried Garlic (see Note, page 82)
1 tablespoon light soy sauce
1 tablespoon sugar cane syrup or cane syrup
sliced spring onion (scallion), to garnish
chilli flakes, to garnish
lime wedges, to serve

METHOD

In a large bowl, whisk together the besan and 1 litre (34 fl oz/4 cups) cold water until smooth. Leave to settle overnight.

Ladle the liquid from the top of the besan mixture into a saucepan. Place over low heat and cook for 15 minutes, stirring or whisking so it doesn't go lumpy.

Now begin to add a few tablespoons of the remaining besan mixture every 2 minutes for the next 15 minutes, whisking or stirring often, until all the mixture is incorporated. The liquid will get thicker and thicker.

Meanwhile, place a frying pan over low heat. Add the peanut oil and sauté the turmeric, shallot, garlic and ginger for 15 minutes. Now add the tomato, paprika, chicken and a pinch of sea salt. Stir-fry over medium heat for 10 minutes, or until the chicken is cooked. Remove from the heat and set aside.

Briefly blanch the baby bok choy in boiling water, drain and set aside.

Toast the sesame seeds in a frying pan over medium heat until fragrant. Remove from the heat and set aside.

To serve, divide the noodles among four soup bowls. Ladle the besan mixture over the noodles, then top with the chicken mixture. Top each bowl with the bok choy, bean sprouts, sesame seeds, peanuts, fried garlic, soy sauce and sugar cane syrup.

Garnish with spring onion and chilli flakes and serve with lime wedges.

MYANMAR

Kengtung was our last stop in Myanmar, before heading off to Thailand. I was drawn there by the laidback lifestyle, the hill tribe villages and the absence of tourists. Kengtung is the second largest town in the Shan state. Built on the shores of Nawng Tung Lake, it is surrounded by mountains. Its architecture ranges from ancient temples and monasteries and mouldering colonial houses to nondescript modern structures.

Kengtung

Kengtung is the centre for the Kung minority group, which makes up about 80 per cent of the town's population. The name 'Kengtung' means 'Walled City of Tung' and refers to the mythical founder of the city. The region around the city was once tied to the Lanna Kingdom of northern Thailand, and there are many similarities between the two today.

It is the hill tribe people who make this area so fascinating. The completely self-sufficient Anh hill tribe village I wanted to visit was high up in the mountains, but monsoon mudslides made the tricky trip much slower. We reached the village after four hours of driving and were greeted by a village elder named Aye, who was also the village shaman – a healer of the sick. Aye was in his nineties; he had dark leathery skin and jet-black teeth. He told me I had horrible white teeth and that I should rub black bark on them to make them more presentable.

Aye used to go on hunting trips into the jungle and said they were sometimes out there for weeks, so naturally it was important that they took some long-lasting food supplies to sustain them. You'll find out more about his amazing traditional jungle-hunting recipe on page 98.

Back in town, the main market is the lifeblood of Kengtung. I'm sure the local food vendors hadn't seen many foreigners before as they were keen for us to sample everything they had on offer: curries, pastes, soups, sweet puddings, and even buffalo skin that had been charred, boiled, then tossed in a salad of banana blossom and snake beans. But one dish was a standout, made of shredded young bamboo shoots, wrapped around a mixture of finely chopped pork, garlic, chilli and ginger leaves, then flash-fried. It was crunchy, soft and chewy all at the same time. You'll find this wonderful recipe on page 97.

That day, I also learnt an important Myanmar custom. When visiting a Myanmar family, always bring bamboo as a gift. Bamboo grows strong and tall and is very durable, a symbol of the family's unity, growth, strength and good health.

INGREDIENTS

1 fresh banana blossom heart (glossary)
2 tablespoons peanut oil
3 garlic cloves, diced
3 red Asian shallots, sliced
½ teaspoon ground turmeric
½ teaspoon sweet paprika
1 ripe tomato, chopped
1 teaspoon sea salt
1 red chilli, sliced
80 g (3 oz) dried buffalo skin, sliced
2 snake (yard-long) beans, sliced
3 garlic chives, sliced
1 Indian root (glossary), sliced, or 1 baby leek or pencil leek, white part only, sliced
40 g (1½ oz/¼ cup) roasted crushed unsalted peanuts, plus extra to garnish
coriander (cilantro), to garnish

WARM BUFFALO SKIN SALAD

SERVES 4 as part of a shared meal

Buffalo skin is considered a delicacy by the ethnic minority groups of Myanmar. Cooking this dish with Maiher, a village elder, was the very first time I had tried it, and I actually really enjoyed its texture. The buffalo skin itself didn't have much flavour, but it absorbed and carried the flavours that were combined with it.

If you can't get your hands on buffalo skin, use cooked shredded pork skin instead; you can find this refrigerated at your local Vietnamese market, where it is called 'da bi'. If you are using da bi, you don't need to boil it – just toss it with the other ingredients as it is already cooked and ready to go.

METHOD

Peel away and discard the outer leaves from the banana blossom heart. Cook the banana blossom heart in a saucepan of boiling water for 15 minutes, or until tender. Strain, slice finely and set aside.

Heat a frying pan over medium heat. Add the peanut oil and sauté the garlic and shallot until fragrant.

Add the turmeric and paprika and sauté for 3 minutes. Now add the tomato, salt, chilli and buffalo skin and stir-fry for a further 3 minutes.

Meanwhile, place the banana blossom, snake beans, garlic chives, Indian root or leek and the peanuts in a large mixing bowl. Toss together well, then add the hot ingredients from the pan. Mix well.

Transfer the mixture to a serving bowl. Serve garnished with coriander and some extra crushed peanuts.

The food at Kengtung's local markets was like a long banquet: rows of tables were filled with all manner of dishes, ranging from small snacks to colourful curry pastes and dips, to main meals ready-cooked and packaged. I visited during monsoon season, when bamboo grows abundantly, and one unusual-looking dish I really liked was shredded young bamboo shoots, stuffed with pork and flash-fried.

Bamboo is such a versatile plant, and a very sustainable one too. It can grow up to one metre (three feet) overnight, and the fresh shoots are absolutely delicious.

INGREDIENTS

2 small fresh young bamboo shoots, tough outer layer discarded
100 g (3½ oz) minced (ground) pork
1 green chilli, sliced
1 red chilli, sliced
3 garlic cloves, diced
2 ginger leaves (glossary), finely sliced, optional
vegetable oil, for deep-frying
Sticky Rice (page 166), to serve

YOUNG BAMBOO SHOOTS STUFFED WITH PORK & GINGER LEAF

SERVES 4 as a snack or starter

METHOD

Place the bamboo shoots in a saucepan, cover with plenty of cold water and bring to the boil. Allow to boil for 1 hour, or until tender. Drain and leave to cool.

Lay the bamboo shoots on a chopping board. Hold the thick end of one shoot with one hand. With your other hand, quickly run two toothpicks down the shoot, starting 1 cm (½ inch) from the thick end, down to the tip, creating fine thin shreds. Repeat with the other shoot.

Place the pork, chillies, garlic and a pinch of sea salt on a large chopping board and pile into a mound. Using two sharp knives or cleavers, mince all these ingredients together.

Place one heaped tablespoon of the pork filling in the middle of one bamboo shoot. Sprinkle some ginger leaf on top, then close up the parcel, securing it with bamboo rope or kitchen string. Repeat with the remaining ingredients.

Half-fill a medium-sized wok with vegetable oil and heat to 180°C (350°F), or until a cube of bread dropped into the oil browns in 15 seconds. Add the bamboo shoots one at a time and deep-fry for 3–4 minutes on each side, or until golden brown and crisp. Drain briefly on paper towels.

Cut the bamboo shoots in half and serve with sticky rice.

INGREDIENTS

200 g (7 oz) dried smoked beef (glossary) or Chinese beef jerky
2 tablespoons vegetable oil
2 garlic cloves, finely sliced
3 red Asian shallots, sliced
3 cm (1¼ inch) piece of fresh ginger, peeled and julienned
5 cm (2 inch) piece of fresh galangal, peeled and sliced
1 lemongrass stem, white part only, finely sliced
1 teaspoon ground turmeric
½ teaspoon sweet paprika
2 red chillies, sliced
8 makrut (kaffir lime) leaves, julienned
1 spring onion (scallion), sliced
4 saw-tooth coriander (cilantro) leaves (glossary), sliced
Sticky Rice (page 166) or steamed jasmine rice, to serve

AROMATIC STIR-FRIED SMOKED BEEF

SERVES 4 as part of a shared meal

I hitched a ride on top of an old jeep to a small village occupied by the Anh ethnic minority, where I met Aye, the village shaman. The first thing he said is that I have horrible teeth. He told me they were too white and that I should rub them with black bark every day so they turn black. "Only animals and beasts have white teeth," he said.

I didn't heed his dental advice, but I did take his advice on a traditional Anh dish his mother used to cook. When the men headed into the jungle on long hunting trips, they also took non-perishable foods in the form of dried smoked beef, aromatics, roots and powders, which they would cook up with the wild herbs and vegetables they foraged along the way. And so this dish was born.

If you can't find smoked beef, thick beef jerky or finely sliced beef sirloin are good substitutes.

METHOD

Put the dried beef in a saucepan, cover with plenty of cold water and bring to the boil. Allow to boil for 30 minutes, or until softened. Drain well, reserving 250 ml (8½ fl oz/1 cup) of the cooking liquid. Allow the beef to cool, then slice finely and set aside.

Heat a frying pan or wok over medium-high heat. Add the vegetable oil and sauté the garlic and shallot until fragrant. Now add the ginger, galangal, lemongrass, turmeric, paprika, chilli and a pinch of sea salt. Stir in the beef and the reserved cooking liquid, reduce the heat to medium-low and simmer for 4 minutes.

Stir in the makrut leaves and spring onion. Garnish with the coriander and serve with sticky rice or jasmine rice.

HIGH UP IN THE MOUNTAINS, THE ANH HILL TRIBE IS A MODEL OF SELF-SUFFICIENCY, AND THE PEOPLE ARE HAPPY TO SHARE THEIR LOCAL WISDOM

Travelling during monsoon season, we had to endure torrential rain, severe heat and humidity, as well as hotel air-conditioning. Most of us came down with a cold at some stage, so I was always looking out for tasty but medicinal traditional dishes.

One morning I woke up feeling under the weather, but as soon as I cooked up this light, subtle and very flavoursome soup I felt a whole lot better. It just felt so good to eat. A lot of the soup's flavour comes from the dried fermented soya beans used by the local mountain ethnic groups. If you can't get any, use the preserved bean curd sold in glass jars at your local Asian market. A teaspoon would do the job.

INGREDIENTS

2 whole lemongrass stems
1 teaspoon sea salt
2 red chillies, chopped
4 apple eggplants (aubergines; see Note), cut into quarters
12 pea eggplants (aubergines; see Note)
1 Japanese eggplant (aubergine), cut into 2 cm (¾ inch) slices
1 carrot, cut into 1 cm (½ inch) pieces
1 ridged gourd, cut into 2 cm (¾ inch) pieces (glossary)
2 tablespoons soy sauce
1 handful choko leaves
1 handful fish mint leaves or pennywort leaves (glossary)
1 handful sweet basil or water spinach leaves
1 handful safflower leaves or watercress sprigs
4 saw-tooth coriander (cilantro) leaves (glossary), sliced
4 cm (1½ inch) piece of fresh ginger, peeled and julienned
steamed jasmine rice, to serve

SHAN MEDICINAL VEGETABLE SOUP
SERVES 4

METHOD

Smash the lemongrass stems with a heavy cleaver, then tie each one in a knot. Place in a saucepan with 1 litre (34 fl oz/4 cups) water and bring to the boil.

Pound the salt and chilli together using a mortar and pestle, then add to the boiling water. When the water returns to the boil, add the vegetables and soy sauce and boil for 5 minutes, or until the vegetables are tender.

Now stir in all the leaves except the coriander. Reduce the heat to low and simmer for a further 2 minutes.

Transfer to individual bowls and garnish with the coriander and ginger. Serve with jasmine rice.

NOTE

Apple eggplants are green or white and about the size of golf balls. Pea eggplants, also called baby Thai eggplants, are green marble-sized eggplants, sold in clusters like grapes. They are used whole and burst when bitten into. You'll find them both at Asian markets.

MYANMAR–KENGTUNG

INGREDIENTS

1 fresh young bamboo shoot
1 corn cob husk
1 handful lemon basil, sliced
1 tablespoon black sesame seeds, pounded into a powder
2 red Asian shallots, sliced
1 teaspoon Garlic Oil (see Note, page 82)
juice of ½ lime

BAMBOO SALAD
SERVES 4 as part of a shared meal

Throughout the markets of Myanmar, I had seen street vendors selling cooked red bamboo. I was intrigued as to where the red bamboo came from, until a local lady shared the secret with me. She walked me to her cornfield (as you do in Myanmar), and peeled the green husks from a corn cob. She placed them in a pot of water with the young bamboo, brought it to the boil and presto: the water and bamboo turned red!

This magic trick only works with fresh bamboo. If you can't get any, you can use whole bamboo shoots vacuum-packed in brine; these are usually pre-cooked, so they don't need to be boiled, and won't turn red.

METHOD

Cut away and discard the tough outer layer of the bamboo shoot, then cut the shoot into quarters lengthways. Place in a saucepan with the corn husk, cover with plenty of cold water and bring to the boil. Allow to boil for 30 minutes, or until the bamboo becomes a light red colour. (The corn husk is what makes the bamboo turn red - see introduction.)

Drain off the water, then add fresh water and bring to the boil again. Boil for a further 30 minutes, then remove the bamboo and allow to cool.

Run two toothpicks along the length of the bamboo, cutting it into long thin shreds. Now cut the bamboo into 4 cm (1½ inch) lengths and transfer to a mixing bowl.

Add the remaining ingredients and a pinch of sea salt. Mix well and serve.

CHAPTER 3

Thailand
CHIANG KHONG TO CHIANG MAI

Thailand
CHIANG KHONG TO CHIANG MAI

In 1977, my family fled Vietnam by boat to escape the aftermath of the Vietnam War. My father had never steered a boat before, but he had to learn very quickly as it was literally do or die. My brother, sister and mother, who was heavily pregnant with me, were hidden on the bottom deck.

After a few weeks on the ocean, we landed in Malaysia, but we were pushed back out to sea as the Malaysian authorities thought there were too many Vietnamese refugees arriving by boat. One week later, we arrived on the shores of Thailand, where I was eventually born. We stayed in a refugee camp in Din Daeng, just south of Bangkok, for one year before moving to Australia, so I didn't actually have the pleasure of experiencing life in Thailand.

I was a little anxious about returning to my birth country – would I feel like a foreigner, or would it feel like I was coming home?

All I knew of Thailand was that it was South-East Asia's most internationally recognised country, and that the food had always stayed true to its traditions, despite many outside influences. I was there to investigate the northern

cuisine – known to be spicier, punchier and more powerful than the food in the rest of the country.

Northern Thailand is far from monocultural. One of the crossroads of Asia, it has been caught up in regional wars for centuries. The influences of past rulers and immigrants have over time blended in and out of the food, culture, architecture and the bloodlines of the people, making for a most interesting and diverse story among the mountains of northern Thailand.

I started my northern exploration in Chiang Khong, where I hoped to catch a giant catfish and discover the secrets of an authentic tom yum pla. I also wanted to delve into the complexities of the northern-style curry pastes, and learn how to catch my own rice paddy frogs to cook a farmer's frog curry.

I then travelled to the mountains further north, where I visited an Akha village near Mae Salong and prepared a rustic spicy tomato dip with an Akha grandmother using the freshest ingredients. I set up a kitchen in a banana forest and used the heart of a banana trunk to prepare a chicken and banana trunk noodle curry.

My Thai journey ended in the bustling town of Chiang Mai, where I lapped up the nightlife and cooked northern Thai classics such as green papaya salad, barbecued pork belly and warm jackfruit salad.

I also sampled an assortment of crispy insects, which I'm sure will feature in Western fine-dining restaurants some day soon!

PLUCKING RICE STALKS FROM THE WET MUD EXPOSES EELS, FISH, CRABS, SNAKES, FROGS AND MICE – A RICH FEAST FOR FARMERS, WHO COOK THEM UP FOR LUNCH

THAILAND

Chiang Khong faces the Lao border town of Huay Xai, across the Mekong River. Lord Buddha was said to have visited this small sleepy town more than 2500 years ago. Today it relies mainly on fishing.
The Mekong River is the lifeblood of this region, second only to the Amazon River in its diversity of fish. It is the major source of protein for the local people, and fishermen constantly work its rich waters.

Chiang Khong

My first day began early, when I met Mr Ta, famous for catching the town's largest giant catfish. I met him at his home, a stone's throw from the Mekong River. He was in his sixties, dark-skinned and built like a rock. He greeted me with the friendliest smile and placed his arms around my shoulders as we walked down to the river together.

We hopped into his boat and travelled upstream. He fanned his small fishing net into the strong current, and we flowed back downstream a few kilometres before Mr Ta stopped his boat and I pulled the net in. We caught many small fish, which I let go, but then came the big one – an enormous catfish! But Mr Ta played it cool. "Ah, that's nothing," he smiled. "I've caught a catfish weighing 250 kilograms – and giant stingrays too!"

He said he usually cooks his fresh catfish with tom yum, which made me super excited. We foraged through his neighbour's gardens, harvesting fresh ingredients for his broth. Galangal, lemongrass, chilli, makrut (kaffir lime), tomatoes, shallots, saw-tooth coriander (cilantro) – the fresh organic produce that makes this soup what it should be, not the powdered seasonings some Thai restaurants use.

Fresh is key in northern Thai cooking, and I learnt this first hand when I visited a rice paddy field just after harvesting. When the rice stalks are plucked out of the wet muddy ground, the field animals are exposed. That's when the rice farmers catch them and cook them up for lunch.

With the help of one farmer, I caught six frogs and one eel. I let the eel go, but the farmer insisted I cook a 'farmer's rice paddy frog curry'. The spice pastes in northern Thai curries are spicy and pungent, with loads of red chillies, galangal, lemongrass, makrut, shrimp paste and anchovy paste. A real party on the palate.

INGREDIENTS

2 litres (68 fl oz/8 cups) fish stock (see Note)
3 lemongrass stems, white part only, bruised
6 cm (2¼ inch) piece of fresh galangal, finely sliced
7 bird's eye chillies, bruised
5 red Asian shallots, peeled and bruised
8 makrut (kaffir lime) leaves, torn
100 ml (3½ fl oz) fish sauce
400 g (14 oz) catfish or silver perch fillets, cut into 2.5 cm (1 inch) pieces
10 cherry tomatoes, quartered
3 spring onions (scallions), cut into 4 cm (1½ inch) lengths
6 saw-tooth coriander (cilantro) leaves (glossary), sliced
100 ml (3½ fl oz) lime juice
1 handful coriander (cilantro), to garnish
steamed jasmine rice, to serve

TOM YUM PLA SOUP WITH CATFISH
SERVES 4-6

I've sampled many bowls of tom yum soup in Australia, but my Thai friends always said they weren't very authentic. So when I met the most experienced fisherman in Chiang Khong, who says he makes the best tom yum soup, I had to cook with him and learn. Together we foraged through his neighbour's gardens – everything was either plucked off a tree or dug out of the ground. And the fish – well I proudly caught that one myself! Mr Ta's recipe calls for seven bird's eye chillies, but if you are not Thai, I strongly suggest cutting that amount by half.

METHOD

Pour the stock into a stockpot or large saucepan. Add the lemongrass, galangal, chillies, shallots and makrut leaves and bring to the boil. Reduce the heat and simmer for 5 minutes. Add the fish sauce, fish and cherry tomatoes and bring back to the boil. Skim off any impurities.

Reduce the heat to low and simmer for 6 minutes, or until the fish is just cooked. Stir in the spring onion, saw-tooth coriander and lime juice. Garnish with coriander and serve with steamed jasmine rice.

NOTE

To make fish stock, place 1 kg (2 lb 3 oz) fish trimmings (bones, head and tail) in a large saucepan with 4 halved garlic cloves, a chopped 2 cm (¾ inch) piece of fresh ginger, 1 bashed lemongrass stem, 2 makrut (kaffir lime) leaves, 2 chopped spring onions (scallions) and 2 litres (68 fl oz/8 cups) water. Bring to the boil, skim off the impurities, then simmer for 30 minutes, skimming constantly. Pour the stock through a fine sieve and cool. Portion into smaller amounts and refrigerate or freeze until required.

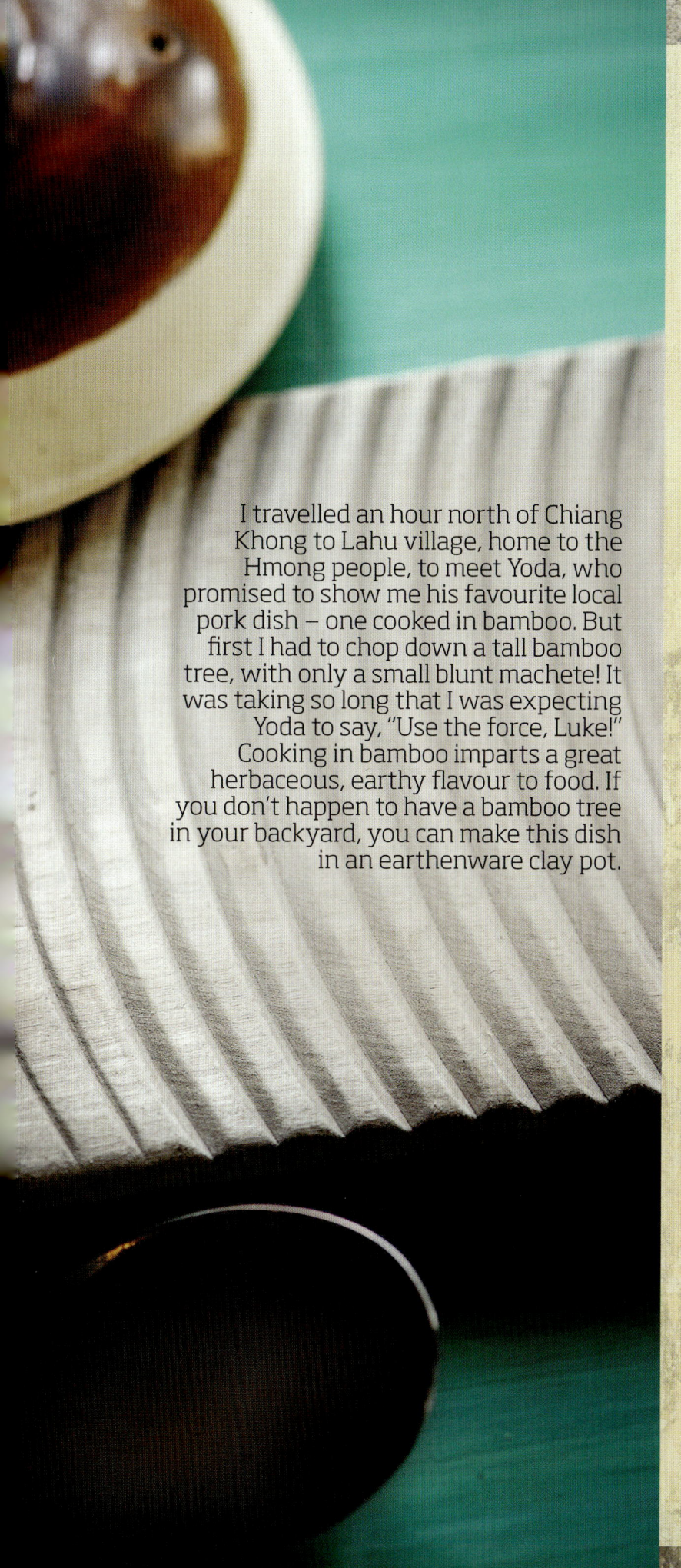

I travelled an hour north of Chiang Khong to Lahu village, home to the Hmong people, to meet Yoda, who promised to show me his favourite local pork dish – one cooked in bamboo. But first I had to chop down a tall bamboo tree, with only a small blunt machete! It was taking so long that I was expecting Yoda to say, "Use the force, Luke!" Cooking in bamboo imparts a great herbaceous, earthy flavour to food. If you don't happen to have a bamboo tree in your backyard, you can make this dish in an earthenware clay pot.

INGREDIENTS
50 cm (20 inch) length of large bamboo, optional
1–2 banana leaves

FILLING
500 g (1 lb 2 oz) pork loin, finely sliced
3 lemongrass stems, white part only, finely chopped
110 g (3½ oz/1 cup) finely chopped red Asian shallots
6 cm (2¼ inch) piece of fresh galangal, peeled and finely sliced
5 dried red chillies, chopped
1 tablespoon sea salt

TO GARNISH
2 makrut (kaffir lime) leaves, finely sliced
1 long red chilli, julienned
1 handful Thai basil leaves

PORK CHARGRILLED IN BAMBOO
SERVES 4 as part of a shared meal

METHOD
In a mixing bowl, combine the filling ingredients and 375 ml (12½ fl oz/1½ cups) water. Mix well.

If using bamboo to cook this dish, open out one end of the bamboo and place the filling inside. Roll up two banana leaves, fold them in half, then use them to close the bamboo opening. Cook the bamboo over a medium-hot charcoal fire, placing the bamboo over the grill at an angle of 45 degrees. Cook for 30 minutes, rotating the bamboo every 10 minutes.

Alternatively, soak the lid and bowl of a clay pot in water for 15 minutes. Place the filling in the clay pot and set it on the stovetop. Bring to the boil, skimming off any impurities, then reduce the heat to medium-low. Cover the surface of the filling with one banana leaf, cutting it to fit as necessary. Cover and cook for 20 minutes.

Empty the pork mixture onto a serving platter. Garnish with the makrut leaves, chilli and basil and serve.

THAILAND – CHIANG KHONG

SECOND ONLY TO THE AMAZON FOR ITS DIVERSITY OF FISH, THE MEKONG IS THE REGION'S LIFEBLOOD. LOCALS WORK ITS FERTILE WATERS FROM DAWN TO DUSK

WOK-TOSSED CATFISH WITH GALANGAL & GREEN PEPPERCORNS

SERVES 4 as part of a shared meal

INGREDIENTS

60 ml (2 fl oz/¼ cup) vegetable oil
500 g (1 lb 2 oz) catfish or silver perch fillets, cut into 2.5 cm (1 inch) pieces
2 lemongrass stems, white part only, finely chopped
5 cm (2 inch) piece of fresh galangal, peeled and finely sliced
8 finger roots (glossary), peeled and finely sliced; alternatively, use some additional fresh galangal or young ginger
3 garlic cloves, finely chopped
1 onion, cut into wedges
10 whole fresh green peppercorns
6 makrut (kaffir limes), finely sliced
2 long red chillies, finely sliced
2 tablespoons fish sauce
2 teaspoons oyster sauce
2 teaspoons sugar
1 tablespoon lime juice
1 handful Thai basil leaves
steamed jasmine rice, to serve

METHOD

Add the vegetable oil to a wok and heat to 180°C (350°F), or until a cube of bread dropped into the oil browns in 15 seconds.

Fry the fish, in two batches, for 3–4 minutes, or until crisp and golden. Remove from the oil and drain on paper towels.

Transfer the hot oil to a metal container to re-use in other recipes, reserving a tablespoon of oil in the wok.

Now add the lemongrass, galangal, finger root, garlic and onion to the wok. Stir-fry for 2 minutes over medium-high heat, or until fragrant.

Return the fish to the wok. Add the peppercorns, makrut slices, chilli, fish sauce, oyster sauce and sugar, then stir-fry for a further 3 minutes.

Sprinkle with the lime juice and transfer to a serving plate. Garnish with the basil and serve with steamed jasmine rice.

This recipe also belongs to Mr Ta, the great fisherman from Chiang Khong who helped me catch a 12 kg (26 lb 4 oz) catfish from the Mekong River.
And it was he who introduced me to finger root, known in Thailand as 'krachai'. This rhizome gets its name from its shape, as it looks like many little fingers. It belongs to the same family as ginger and galangal, but is much milder in flavour. If you can't get fresh finger root, you can find it preserved in jars at your local Asian market.

RICE PADDY FROG CURRY

SERVES 4 as part of a shared meal

INGREDIENTS

- 2 frogs, skinned, cleaned and butterflied
- 100 ml (3½ fl oz) vegetable oil
- 3 garlic cloves, smashed
- 2 snake (yard-long) beans, cut into 2 cm (¾ inch) lengths
- 3 wing beans, cut into 2 cm (¾ inch) lengths
- 10 pea eggplants (aubergines; see Note, page 103)
- 4 fresh betel leaves (glossary), torn
- 1 handful ivy gourd or pennywort leaves (glossary)
- 4 sasbania flowers (glossary), stamen removed, or 4 pumpkin (squash) or zucchini (courgette) flowers
- 4 makrut (kaffir lime) leaves, torn
- 5 bird's eye chillies, smashed
- 1 tablespoon fish sauce

THAI CHILLI PASTE

- 3 tablespoons finely chopped lemongrass, white part only (about 2 stems)
- 3 tablespoons finely chopped fresh galangal
- 4 makrut (kaffir lime) leaves, finely sliced
- 4 tablespoons finely chopped garlic
- 4 tablespoons finely chopped red Asian shallots
- 13 dried chillies, finely chopped
- 1 tablespoon shrimp paste
- 2 tablespoons mam ruoc (Vietnamese fermented shrimp paste; glossary)

TO GARNISH

- 1 tablespoon sliced spring onion (scallion)
- 1 tablespoon sliced coriander (cilantro)
- 2 sasbania, pumpkin (squash) or zucchini (courgette) flowers

METHOD

Heat a barbecue chargrill or chargrill pan to medium. Chargrill the frogs for 10 minutes on each side. Chop off the feet, then chop each frog into eight pieces.

To make the Thai chilli paste, add each ingredient, one at a time, to a large mortar or food processor. Pound with a pestle or process each ingredient well before adding the next one; keep pounding until a smooth paste forms and all the ingredients are well incorporated. Transfer 2 tablespoons of the chilli paste to a bowl; seal the rest in a clean screw-top jar and refrigerate for use in other Thai recipes.

Add a few tablespoons of water to the mortar, cleaning both the mortar and pestle with the water. Pour the water out and reserve it for the curry.

Add the vegetable oil to a hot wok. Add the garlic and the reserved 2 tablespoons of chilli paste and sauté over medium-high heat for 3 minutes, or until fragrant.

Now add the frog meat and stir-fry for 2 minutes, then add the beans and eggplants and stir-fry for a further 2 minutes.

Add the betel and ivy gourd leaves, sasbania flowers and reserved chilli paste water. Stir-fry for 1 minute, then add the makrut leaves, chillies and fish sauce. Stir-fry for a further minute.

Transfer to a serving platter. Garnish with spring onion, coriander and your choice of flowers and serve.

Frog meat is tender, delicious, high in protein, low in fat – and an aphrodisiac, Thai men tell me. I had a fantastic time catching my own frogs. When rice farmers pluck their rice stalks out of the paddies, all the wild animals – eels, snakes, field crabs and field mice – are left exposed, ready to be caught and eaten. But if you can't catch your own frogs, you can use quails here instead. The curries of northern Thailand are not the heavy coconut cream curries found in the centre. The northern style is drier, with loads more chilli in the paste.

THAILAND – CHIANG KHONG

THAILAND

Mae Salong was the last bastion for renegade Chinese soldiers fighting Mao's Communist regime. When the conflict ended in the early 1980s, the Chinese rebels were allowed to stay. They helped the local ethnic communities transform Mae Salong from a renegade camp into a tourist village. As part of this process, opium production was successfully substituted with mountain produce such as mushrooms, and above all oolong tea, which is now the region's main crop.

Mae Salong

For decades the hill tribe farmers relied on opium crops for their income. The King of Thailand, in his wisdom, set out to eradicate this illicit trade, which was detrimental not only to the people of Thailand, but to the rest of the world. This fantastic project is known as the Royal Project. Seeing first hand the transformation that has taken place, I understand why the Thai people have so much respect and love for their king and the entire royal family.

The Royal Project has introduced plum, pear and peach trees and 50 varieties of vegetables to the region. More than 274 villages participate in the project, including the village I visited, Mae Salong – home to the Akha people, the dominant ethnic group of this area.

Walking into the picturesque village, the first thing I noticed were the bright red and green chillies drying on the roofs of the huts in the sun, and the impressive traditional silver headpieces the women wore, dressed with red tassels and old Indian rupees. A village elder named Arpeh was keen to show me her headpiece and cook her local specialty – a spicy tomato dip with organic vegetables.

Arpeh lit a handful of dried corn husks for fuel. We took some chillies from her roof and picked tomatoes, garlic and shallots from her garden, threaded them onto bamboo skewers and grilled them over the burning husks. Once blackened, I peeled off the skins and pounded the flesh in a mortar, adding fermented soya bean sheets. It was the most rustic, delicious and simple vegetarian dish I'd ever made, with a divinely sweet smokiness.

Another Mae Salong specialty is pork hocks, slowly braised with star anise, cassia bark, sugar cane and young coconut juice – a Chinese-influenced dish served as street food. When I finally convinced the film crew to try it, they were speechless. We sat by the side of the road eating in silence. Everyone ordered seconds, and we dined on it for days.

TO SERVE

finely sliced white cabbage

raw choko, peeled and cut into batons

raw mustard greens, leaves cut in half crossways, with the bottom halves cut into thin wedges through the stems

TOMATO DIP

5 long red chillies

4 garlic cloves, skin left on

4 red Asian shallots, skin left on

3 vine-ripened tomatoes

1 dried fermented bean curd sheet (glossary), or 1 teaspoon preserved bean curd, squashed to a paste

SPICY TOMATO DIP WITH RAW SEASONAL VEGETABLES

SERVES 4 as part of a shared meal

The Akha are the dominant ethnic group of Mae Salong, originally from Tibet and now living in Myanmar and northern Thailand. I was there to meet Arpeh, a village elder who was going to show me a traditional Akha dish. I must admit I was expecting to go hunting for wild boar or goat in the mountains, but instead we made an amazing vegetarian dish, using vegetables grown organically in the village garden.

Much of the flavour of this dish comes from the dried fermented bead curd sheet. If you can't get any, use the preserved bean curd packed in glass jars at your Asian market.

METHOD

To make the tomato dip, first heat a barbecue chargrill or chargrill pan to medium-low. Chargrill the chillies for about 3 minutes, turning often until they darken in colour. Remove from the heat. Now chargrill the garlic, shallots and tomatoes until blackened and tender. Remove from the heat and allow to cool.

If using the bean curd sheet, cook it on the grill for 1 minute on each side, or until crisp. Remove from the heat.

Peel the blackened garlic, shallots and tomatoes. Place in a large mortar with the chillies, bean curd and a pinch of sea salt, then pound with a pestle into a smooth paste.

Transfer to a bowl and use as a dip with your choice of raw seasonal vegetables.

NORTHERN THAI CUISINE IS FAMOUS FOR ITS STRONG, SPICY PUNCH; IN MAE SALONG WE FOUND HUNDREDS OF RED AND GREEN CHILLIES DRYING UNDER THE SUN

BANANA TRUNK & CHICKEN CURRY

SERVES 4

INGREDIENTS

200 g (7 oz) banana trunk heart (glossary), tinned lotus stems, or whole bamboo shoots in brine
juice of 1 lime
2 tablespoons vegetable oil
1 kg (2 lb 3 oz) whole chicken, chopped into bite-sized pieces through the bone
4 makrut (kaffir lime) leaves
1 tablespoon fish sauce
40–50 g (1½–2 oz) bundle of dried glass noodles, soaked in water for 30 minutes, then drained
2 spring onions (scallions), sliced
4 coriander (cilantro) sprigs, sliced

THAI CHILLI PASTE

3 tablespoons finely chopped lemongrass, white part only (about 2 stems)
3 tablespoons finely chopped fresh galangal
4 makrut (kaffir lime) leaves, finely sliced
4 tablespoons finely chopped garlic
4 tablespoons finely chopped red Asian shallots
13 dried chillies, finely chopped
1 tablespoon shrimp paste
2 tablespoons mam ruoc (Vietnamese fermented shrimp paste; glossary)

The versatile banana tree is grown in all tropical regions in Asia. This herbaceous plant gives us the fruit of course, but we can also use the blossoms in salads, and the beautiful long leaves to wrap around foods for steaming or chargrilling. In northern Thailand, the locals also cook the actual banana trunk in curries. The trunk itself doesn't have much flavour, but it acts as a sponge, absorbing other flavours and adding great texture to the dish. If you can't get any, use lotus stems instead.

METHOD

To make the Thai chilli paste, add each ingredient, one at a time, to a large mortar or food processor. Pound with a pestle or process each ingredient well before adding the next one; keep pounding until a smooth paste forms and all the ingredients are well incorporated. Transfer 2 tablespoons of the chilli paste to a bowl; seal the rest in a clean screw-top jar and refrigerate for use in other Thai recipes.

Add a few tablespoons of water to the mortar, cleaning both the mortar and pestle with the water. Pour the water out and reserve it for the curry.

If using the banana trunk hearts, slice them into 5 cm (2 inch) lengths, then cut into quarters. Place them in a water bath with the lime juice to stop them discolouring. Set aside. If using lotus stems or bamboo shoots, cut them into 4 cm (1½ inch) lengths and set aside.

Add the vegetable oil to a hot wok. Add the reserved 2 tablespoons of chilli paste and sauté over medium-high heat for 3 minutes, or until fragrant. Add the chicken and stir-fry for a further 3 minutes.

Now add the reserved chilli paste water from the mortar, plus enough extra water to just cover the chicken. Bring to the boil, skimming off any impurities that rise to the surface. Add the banana trunk, lotus stems or bamboo shoots and cook for 6–8 minutes, or until the chicken is cooked and the banana trunk becomes soft.

Now add the makrut leaves, fish sauce and noodles and cook for a further minute.

Garnish with the spring onion and coriander and serve.

SLOW-BRAISED PORK HOCKS

SERVES 4

INGREDIENTS

- 2 fresh pork hocks
- vegetable oil, for deep-frying
- 4 coriander (cilantro) roots, scraped clean and chopped
- 4 garlic cloves, crushed
- 10 white peppercorns, crushed
- 6 cm (2¼ inch) piece of fresh ginger, sliced
- 2 black cardamom pods (glossary), bruised
- 3 star anise
- 5 cm (2 inch) piece of cassia bark
- 1 tablespoon liquid palm sugar (glossary), or shaved dark palm sugar (jaggery)
- 60 ml (2 fl oz/¼ cup) light soy sauce
- 2 tablespoons dark soy sauce
- 50 ml (2 fl oz) chicken stock (page 23)
- 1 litre (34 fl oz/4 cups) young coconut juice (glossary)
- 1 handful coriander (cilantro) leaves
- steamed jasmine rice, to serve

We were in the northern mountains of Mae Salong, it was 2pm, and the crew were tired and hungry. I found a row of street-food stalls offering offal, offal and more offal. I was in heaven, but the others would rather go hungry! Then I saw a lady with an oversized wok slow-braising pork hocks in a lovely aromatic, amber-coloured broth. You'd think the crew would be excited, but no, they were reluctant as they had never tried it. I wasn't taking no for an answer – and they ended up loving it so much they ate it for the next three days!

Pork hock is the rear leg of the pig; it is inexpensive, robust in flavour and has great texture. Please take the time to cook it, as it is well worth the effort.

METHOD

Place the hocks in a saucepan with enough cold salted water to cover. Boil for 3 minutes, skimming off any impurities. Drain, wash under cold water, then drain again and pat dry.

Half-fill a wok or large saucepan with vegetable oil and heat to 180°C (350°F), or until a cube of bread dropped into the oil browns in 15 seconds. Add the hocks and cook for 3 minutes on each side, or until lightly browned. The oil can spit violently, so cover the wok with a splatter guard if the oil spits too much. Remove the hocks and drain.

Heat 1 tablespoon of the deep-frying oil in a saucepan. Stir-fry the coriander roots, garlic, peppercorns and ginger over medium-high heat until fragrant. Add the cardamom, star anise and cassia and fry for a further minute.

Add the sugar, soy sauces, stock and coconut juice. Bring to the boil. Add the hocks, and a little water if needed to cover them. Bring back to the boil and skim off any impurities. Reduce the heat, slightly cover with a lid, then simmer for 3½–4 hours, or until the meat begins to fall off the bone.

Serve garnished with coriander, with steamed jasmine rice.

THAILAND

Home to almost a million people, Chiang Mai is northern Thailand's largest city, and culturally its most significant. Founded in 1296, among the highest mountains in the country, Chiang Mai is located on the Ping River, 700 kilometres north of Bangkok. Its name means 'new city', as it succeeded Chiang Rai as the capital of the Lanna Kingdom.

Chiang Mai is at its best after sunset. Busy city streets are transformed into colourful, bustling night markets, jam-packed with the thing closest to my heart and theirs – food.

Chiang Mai

My first stop was the Warorot night market, a Thai foodie paradise. Thais are obsessed with food, and that food must be fresh, tasty and accessible. Locals come to Warorot for a quick, cheap dinner, and ride their motorbikes through crowds of pedestrians to pick up takeaway. As soon as I arrived, a huge burst of energy hit me: I wanted to eat everything I saw. The first thing that lured me in was the smoky aroma of chargrilled pork belly. I asked several cooks what their marinade was and received a few different answers, so I had to cook my own to compare the versions.

I just adore Thai hospitality: vendors let me use their bench space, sauces and seasonings. When I had my marinated pork belly on the grill, I hopped over to a cart selling shaved green papaya to make the much-loved som tum. There are many versions of the green papaya salad, particularly in Vietnam, Laos and Thailand, each with their own unique seasonings and additions. I find the Thai version the best: it is incredibly spicy, but the balance of sweet, sour and salty, along with the amazing texture, is absolutely perfect.

The lady who owned the green papaya cart had been selling the salad at the Warorot market for 20 years, so I respected anything she said. She suggested I go to the early-morning market and try the large variety of insects Chiang Mai has to offer. This didn't sound as appetising as chargrilled pork belly or green papaya salad with tamarind snake beans, but to fully immerse myself in Thai cuisine and culture, I needed to eat the unusual foods too. Northern Thais have been eating bugs and insects for centuries, as they are a great source of protein for field workers.

I found a stall serving an assortment of insects, deep-fried and tossed with pandan leaves and chilli. I was initially a bit hesitant, but as soon as the first one slipped down, I had no problem trying the rest. Water cockroaches, mole crickets, cicadas, bamboo worms and grasshoppers: they were all delicious. I came to the conclusion that we should stop eating so much meat and start eating more insects for protein. Our animals would live a longer, happier life and we would use fewer pesticides on our crops!

South-East Asians love to eat unripened fruits, as they are crunchy and have both sweet and sour notes. Thai people adore green mango, green guava, green figs and especially green papaya – the most popular green fruit of all, served in a salad in every market, street stall or restaurant. There are many variations of the green papaya salad. This version was taught to me by a cute lady who had a little som tum cart at the local Chiang Mai night market. Warning: if you are not Thai or married to one, only put two chillies in the salad!

INGREDIENTS

1 garlic clove, sliced
1 tablespoon unsalted roasted peanuts
4 bird's eye chillies
4 snake (yard-long) beans, cut into 3 cm (1¼ inch) lengths
1 tablespoon shaved palm sugar (jaggery)
5 cherry tomatoes, cut in half
200 g (7 oz) shredded green papaya
2 tablespoons Tamarind Water (see Note, page 85)
1 tablespoon lime juice
2 tablespoons fish sauce
lime wedges, to serve

GREEN PAPAYA SALAD
SERVES 4 as part of a shared meal

METHOD

Using a large mortar and pestle, pound the garlic into a paste. Add the peanuts and chillies and pound until mixed with the garlic.

Now add the snake beans, gently pounding while adding the palm sugar, tomatoes and papaya. Continue gently pounding and mixing with a spoon at the same time.

Next add the tamarind water, lime juice and fish sauce. Lightly pound and mix for a further minute, for all the flavours to infuse.

Transfer to a bowl and serve straight away with the lime wedges.

THAILAND – CHIANG MAI

INGREDIENTS

1 young jackfruit, about 1 kg (2 lb 3 oz), or 500 g (1 lb 2 oz) drained tinned jackfruit
2 tablespoons Thai Chilli Paste (page 131)
2 tablespoons vegetable oil
2 garlic cloves, diced
4 makrut (kaffir lime) leaves, finely sliced
5 cherry tomatoes, quartered
1 teaspoon fish sauce
4 coriander (cilantro) sprigs, sliced
2 spring onions (scallions), sliced
Sticky Rice (page 166), to serve

WARM YOUNG JACKFRUIT SALAD

SERVES 4 as part of a shared meal

This dish is cooked on 16 April every year to offer to the temples, to bring good luck and good health. While I was in Chiang Mai, I heard news that my grandmother in Saigon was very ill. I couldn't be there for her, so I went to the oldest temple in Chiang Mai and cooked this dish for her, offered it to the monks and prayed. My grandma is no longer with us, but I am glad I got to communicate with her through food and prayer.

Jackfruit is the world's largest tree-born fruit; however, this dish uses young jackfruit, which develops an artichoke-like flavour when cooked. (If you can't find fresh young jackfruit, buy the tinned flesh at your local Asian market.) Be sure to oil your knife before slicing into the jackfruit, as it releases a sticky sap that will stick to your knife and make slicing difficult.

METHOD

Leaving the skin on the fresh jackfruit, slice it into pieces about 3 cm (1¼ inches) thick. Place in a saucepan of water and boil for 30 minutes, or until tender.

Drain the jackfruit well. Leave to cool, then remove the skin. Cut the flesh into small pieces and set aside.

Put the Thai chilli paste in a large mortar. Gradually add the jackfruit flesh, pounding with a pestle until well incorporated.

Add the vegetable oil to a hot wok. Add the garlic and the jackfruit mixture and stir-fry over medium heat for 3–4 minutes, or until fragrant. Stir in the makrut leaves, tomatoes, fish sauce, coriander and spring onion.

Transfer to a serving bowl, or wrap in a banana leaf parcel. Serve with sticky rice.

CHIANG MAI NOODLE CURRY
SERVES 4

INGREDIENTS
60 ml (2 fl oz/¼ cup) coconut cream
2 tablespoons shaved palm sugar (jaggery)
2 tablespoons soy sauce
400 g (14 oz) boneless, skinless chicken thighs
250 ml (8½ fl oz/1 cup) young coconut juice (glossary)
500 ml (17 fl oz/2 cups) coconut milk
vegetable oil, for deep-frying
700 g (1 lb 9 oz) fresh flat egg noodles
2 spring onions (scallions), finely sliced
1 handful coriander (cilantro) sprigs

SPICE PASTE
2 dried red chillies, soaked in hot water for 10 minutes, then drained and chopped
4 red Asian shallots, chopped
4 garlic cloves, chopped
2 cm (¾ inch) piece of fresh turmeric, peeled and sliced
4 cm (1½ inch) piece of fresh ginger, peeled and sliced
4 coriander (cilantro) roots, scraped clean and chopped
2 teaspoons shrimp paste
2 teaspoons Thai curry powder

Another very popular dish in Chiang Mai is this noodle curry, known as 'kow soi'. We couldn't get permission to film this dish in the heritage-listed location we were originally hoping for – but I did get to cook and sample many bowls of the noodle curry, so here is my favourite version.
This recipe uses Thai curry powder – a fragrant blend of ground pepper, cloves, coriander seeds, cumin, fennel, chilli flakes, turmeric and ginger, available from spice shops and Asian markets.

METHOD
To make the spice paste, blend the chilli, shallot, garlic, turmeric, ginger, coriander roots and shrimp paste into a fine paste, using a large mortar and pestle or a food processor. Mix the curry powder through and set aside.

Pour the coconut cream into a wok and simmer over medium heat for 5 minutes. Add the spice paste and stir until fragrant.

Now add the palm sugar, soy sauce and chicken, mixing until the chicken is coated with all the ingredients.

Stir in the coconut juice, coconut milk and 250 ml (8½ fl oz/1 cup) water. Bring to the boil, skimming off any impurities that rise to the surface. Reduce the heat and simmer for 30 minutes, or until the chicken is tender.

Meanwhile, half-fill a wok or large saucepan with vegetable oil and heat to 180°C (350°F), or until a cube of bread dropped into the oil browns in 15 seconds. Slowly slide about 100 g (3½ oz) of the noodles into the wok and fry for 30 seconds, or until crisp. Remove and drain on paper towels. Set aside.

Bring a saucepan of water to the boil. Divide the remaining noodles into four portions. Blanch each portion separately in the boiling water for 20 seconds, then remove and refresh in iced water – this allows the noodles to develop a nice firmness. Return them to the boiling water for another 10 seconds, then divide among four serving bowls.

Ladle the chicken and curry sauce over the noodles. Garnish with the crisp noodles, spring onion and coriander and serve.

I FOUND A STALL SERVING AN ARRAY OF DEEP-FRIED INSECTS TOSSED WITH PANDAN LEAVES AND CHILLI. AS SOON AS I TRIED ONE, I HAD NO PROBLEM TRYING THE REST

INGREDIENTS

4 garlic cloves, diced
4 coriander (cilantro) roots, scraped clean and finely sliced
2 tablespoons coriander seeds
½ teaspoon sugar
2 tablespoons light soy sauce
60 ml (2 fl oz/¼ cup) oyster sauce
½ teaspoon freshly ground black pepper
400 g (14 oz) piece of pork belly, bone removed

TAMARIND DIPPING SAUCE

125 ml (4 fl oz/½ cup) Tamarind Water (see Note, page 85)
1 tablespoon fish sauce
1 teaspoon caster (superfine) sugar
½ teaspoon pounded fresh galangal
½ teaspoon pounded garlic
½ teaspoon chilli flakes
1 tablespoon finely sliced coriander (cilantro)

CHARGRILLED CHIANG MAI PORK BELLY

SERVES 2 as a meal, or 4 as part of a shared meal

Chiang Mai is at its best after the sun sets, as the night markets come alive. The energy is buzzing, the aromas and colours trap you there for hours, and it's the perfect place to discover true authentic Thai cooking.

I learnt a lot from the cooks at the night markets: I moved from one barbecue stall to another, picking their brains trying to get the perfect marinade for their chargrilled pork belly.

This is the recipe I ended up with after talking to four different cooks. I decided to prepare this dish among all the action of the night markets. It was so much fun – I felt like a real local.

Try to buy your pork belly from an Asian butcher and ask them for young pork belly, suitable for chargrilling. For the very best flavour, marinate it overnight.

METHOD

Using a large mortar and pestle, pound the garlic, coriander roots and coriander seeds to a fine paste. Transfer the paste to a large mixing bowl, stir in the sugar, soy sauce, oyster sauce and pepper and mix to dissolve the sugar. Add the pork and coat it all over. Cover and marinate in the refrigerator for at least 1 hour, or overnight for the best result.

Bring water to a rapid boil in a steamer, wok or large saucepan that will hold a steamer basket. Transfer the pork to a steamer basket or bamboo steamer and place over the pan of boiling water. Cover and steam for 30-40 minutes. Remove from the heat and allow the pork to cool slightly.

Heat a barbecue chargrill or chargrill pan to medium-high. Cut the pork into slices 1 cm (½ inch) thick, then chargrill on each side for 3 minutes, or until cooked through.

Meanwhile, mix the tamarind dipping sauce ingredients in a small bowl until well combined. Cut the pork into 2 cm (¾ inch) pieces and serve hot, with the dipping sauce.

CHAPTER 4

Laos
VIENTIANE TO 4000 ISLANDS

Laos
VIENTIANE TO 4000 ISLANDS

Lao People's Democratic Republic, or PDR, is a landlocked country in South-East Asia, bordered by Myanmar and China to the north-west, Vietnam to the east, Cambodia to the south and Thailand to the west. When I arrived in Laos, the locals told me PDR stands for 'Please Don't Rush!' Lao people take time to enjoy the important things in life: when it's time for breakfast, lunch and dinner, everything stops and attention is turned to eating and relaxing.

So I settled back with the locals to take in and enjoy the simpler things in life. Through their food, I began to understand the rustic nature of the country. Lao cuisine is pungent, extremely spicy and ingredient-focused, showing a real respect for food in its raw form, and using available produce in so many interesting ways.

I've been eating Lao food since I was a kid. Growing up in the Sydney suburbs of Cabramatta and Fairfield, I was spoilt for choice. My family would visit a Lao restaurant every time we craved bursts of flavour and spice. My mother loved dishes such as fermented soft-shell crab and green papaya salad. When the order was taken, the waitress would always ask, 'You want medium spicy or Lao spicy?' We would respond in unison, 'Medium spicy'. In Lao terms, 'medium spicy' is *extremely* spicy, and 'Lao spicy' means your whole upper body goes numb and you feel like submerging your head in an ice bath.

I would always order the chargrilled ox tongue; my younger brother, Leroy, loved the Lao pork sausage with sticky rice; and my father was always busy in the kitchen trying to convince the owner to serve us steamed duck embryo egg with Lao beer.

Now that I was actually in the country, I wanted to explore regional Lao cuisine and discover all the weird and wonderful dishes from small towns and ethnic minority villages.

I began my Lao culinary discovery in the nation's capital, Vientiane, where I met Kampoo, a laidback local who showed me secret foodie locations and introduced me to the most unusual ingredients at the wet market. I also tried out their national game, pétanque.

The sleepy country town vibe I experienced in Vientiane continued wherever I went. I quickly made my way to charming Luang Prabang, as I didn't want to miss out on the Lao New Year celebration known as 'Pi Mai'. I'd heard it was basically a week-long water fight that involves the entire town. And indeed it was: I spent most of the daytime soaking wet with water and paint. At night I would escape to the markets and restaurants to discover barbecue dishes, street food, sweet treats and traditional delicacies.

I then made my way down to 4000 Islands, where the Mekong River changes from its usual rich brown to an expanse of soft turquoise water. Here I learnt traditional fishing techniques and how to prepare exciting, authentic local dishes unlike anything I had experienced before.

From what I've seen here, I think this area of the country will be the 'next big thing' in Lao food and travel.

IN LAOS THERE'S A DEFINITE SHIFT IN PACE. LOCALS TAKE TIME TO ENJOY LIFE'S SIMPLE PLEASURES, ESPECIALLY EATING AND RELAXING

LAOS

Vientiane is the laidback capital of Laos, situated along the Mekong River, right on the Thai border. In Vientiane, the people are genuine and down to earth, and the city feels like a small country town. Life here revolves around work, religion and, of course, really good food.
But it seems that things are on the move, with the economy and tourism growing rapidly. High-rise buildings and big fancy hotels are springing up, and luxury cars cruise the streets.

Vientiane

However, it wasn't the town's modernity that attracted me. What did catch my eye was a French-looking monument known as Patuxai – Vientiane's very own Arc de Triomphe, a victory gate symbolising Laos' independence from France. In 1956, the United States donated millions of dollars to Vientiane to build an airstrip; instead the Lao people used the money to build Patuxai – a lovely example of the local attitude.

Not far from Patuxai is Thong Khan Kham market, where I was told I could find many weird and wonderful foods. I've been to many markets, but this one topped it for me. Ladies were walking around with trays on their heads filled with crispy grasshoppers, other vendors sold buckets of bee larvae, chicken heads, innards, live frogs, pig heads, fermented 'century' eggs and, strangest of all, buffalo hides still covered in hair. Kampoo, who liked to be called 'Poo', said buffalo skin was one of his favourite drinking foods.

So I decided to give it a go. Poo also told me to buy some charcoal and to find a big wooden stick to pound the buffalo skin with. With my skin, charcoal and stick in hand, we made our way to the local pétanque field, where Poo challenged me to a game.

Pétanque is the most popular game in Vientiane, introduced to the locals in the late 1800s by the French. A game played by all ages and sexes, it is the only sport in which Laos has made any real impact on the international stage, and it is now included in the Southeast Asian Games.

But first I lit the charcoal, brought it to very high heat, then placed the buffalo skin on the fire until the skin was blackened. After removing the charred skin from the fire, I placed it on a bench and pounded it with my wooden stick until the blackened parts were smashed away from the skin. It was ready to be eaten. The result was a crispy, chewy and soft-textured buffalo skin to snack on while drinking Lao beer. All the pétanque players absolutely loved it. And after beating Poo on my very first pétanque match, I am seriously thinking about going pro!

DUCK BLOOD SALAD

SERVES 4 as part of a shared meal

INGREDIENTS

- 1 tablespoon vegetable oil
- 1 red Asian shallot, chopped
- 100 g (3½ oz) duck liver, cleaned and finely sliced
- 60 ml (2 fl oz/¼ cup) duck blood
- 1 spring onion (scallion), finely sliced
- 1 handful roughly chopped coriander (cilantro)
- 10 mint leaves
- 10 Vietnamese mint leaves
- 1 tablespoon fried red Asian shallots (see Note)
- 1 tablespoon roasted crushed unsalted peanuts
- 1 lime, cut in half

ACCOMPANIMENTS

- 2 bird's eye chillies, sliced
- 2 snake (yard-long) beans, cut into 4 cm (1½ inch) lengths
- 1 handful Thai basil leaves

METHOD

Add the vegetable oil to a hot frying pan and sauté the shallot until fragrant. Add the duck liver and a pinch of sea salt and stir-fry for 2 minutes. Remove from the heat and allow to cool.

In a serving bowl, mix together the duck blood and 125 ml (4 fl oz/½ cup) water.

Tip the liver mixture into a mixing bowl. Add the spring onion, coriander, mint and Vietnamese mint and gently toss. Evenly scatter the mixture over the bowl of duck blood, then garnish with the fried shallots and peanuts.

Now allow the duck blood to set for 15 minutes. Meanwhile, arrange the accompaniments on a separate plate.

Squeeze the lime juice over the salad. Serve with the accompaniments and Lao beer.

NOTE

Fried red Asian shallots are widely available at Asian markets. To make your own, finely slice 200 g (7 oz) red Asian shallots and wash under cold water. Dry the shallot with a cloth, then set aside on paper towels until completely dry. Heat 1 litre (34 fl oz/4 cups) vegetable oil in a wok to 180°C (350°F), or until a cube of bread dropped into the oil browns in 15 seconds. Fry the shallots in small batches until they turn golden brown, then remove with a slotted spoon to a paper towel. They are best eaten freshly fried, but will keep for up to 2 days in an airtight container. The oil they were cooked in can also be re-used.

This dish brought back memories of watching my father in the backyard with his super-sharp cleaver, carefully slitting the duck's neck to draw out the warm blood. Dad would quickly mix the blood with fish sauce to stop it congealing. It wasn't pleasant to watch, but the finished dish was delectable. The texture of duck blood when slightly set is like nothing else, and the fresh ingredients that are combined with it make for such a unique dish, both to prepare and eat.

It is very difficult to purchase fresh duck blood outside Laos or Vietnam, so if you want to try this dish, the only other option is to buy a live duck and extract the blood yourself, remembering to mix a tablespoon of fish sauce into it!

This dish rejuvenates the blood with nutrients. It is also great for hangovers, if you've had too many Lao beers the night before.

INGREDIENTS

4 lemongrass stems, white part only, chopped
1 large handful dill, chopped
2 spring onions (scallions), sliced
800 g (1 lb 12 oz) whole black tilapia or barramundi, gutted and cleaned, but left unscaled
35 g (1¼ oz/¼ cup) sea salt, for coating
Sticky Rice (page 166), to serve
Tamarind Dipping Sauce (page 144), to serve

CHARGRILLED SALT-CRUSTED LEMONGRASS FISH

SERVES 4 as part of a shared meal

Tilapia lives in freshwater ecosystems and is found in great abundance in the Mekong River. It has a mild buttery flavour, is high in protein, has five times less fat than lean pork or beef, and has very firm skin, which makes it ideal for chargrilling.

This dish is found grilling throughout the streets and markets of Vientiane. After stuffing the fish and coating it in salt, local cooks tie the fish between two bamboo sticks before placing it on the chargrill. This keeps the fish enclosed, and also makes it easier to turn over.

Local ladies believe this is the best dish to eat while pregnant.

METHOD

Soak a bamboo skewer in cold water for 30 minutes.

In a mixing bowl, combine the lemongrass, dill and spring onion. Stuff the mixture into the cavity of the fish, then secure the opening using the bamboo skewer. Now rub the whole fish with all the sea salt, coating it well.

Heat a chargrill pan or barbecue chargrill plate to medium–high. Chargrill the fish for 10–15 minutes on each side, or until cooked through – the scales and skin should peel off easily.

Before serving the fish at the table, peel away and discard the scales and skin.

Serve the fish hot, with sticky rice and the dipping sauce.

INGREDIENTS

250 ml (8½ fl oz/1 cup) pork stock (see Note)
200 g (7 oz) lean pork tenderloin, diced
100 g (3½ oz) pork liver, diced
2 handfuls mint leaves
1 handful sliced coriander (cilantro)
4 spring onions (scallions), finely sliced
2 red chillies, sliced, plus extra to garnish
1 tablespoon Toasted Rice Powder (see Note, page 187)
2 tablespoons padek (Laotian fermented fish sauce; glossary) or mam nem (Vietnamese fermented anchovy sauce; glossary)
juice of 1 lime

ACCOMPANIMENTS

1 Lebanese (short) cucumber, sliced
2 apple eggplants (aubergines; see Note, page 103), quartered
4 bitter melon stems (glossary), with leaves
6 Chinese mustard green (glossary) leaves
6 snake (yard-long) beans, cut into 4 cm (1½ inch) lengths
Sticky Rice (page 166), to serve

Lao 'laap' is very similar to the Thai 'laab'. The only difference is that the Lao version has the addition of padek – an essential ingredient in Lao cuisine.
Often known as Laotian fish sauce, padek is made from small freshwater fish, fermented with rice and salt for many months. It is pungent and adds great depth of flavour to a dish. Unlike Thai or Vietnamese fish sauce, padek is unstrained, so it still has chunks of fish through it, along with all its juices. If you can't get padek, use mam nem (Vietnamese fermented anchovy sauce).

PORK LAAP

SERVES 4 as part of a shared meal

METHOD

Pour the stock into a hot wok. When it begins to boil, add the pork meat and liver and cook, stirring, for 2 minutes, or until the meat is cooked.

Transfer the mixture to a mixing bowl and allow to cool for 2 minutes.

Now add the mint, coriander, spring onion, chilli, rice powder, padek or mam nem and lime juice. Mix together well, then transfer to a serving platter. Garnish with some extra chilli slices.

Serve with the raw vegetables and sticky rice.

NOTE

To make pork stock, wash 500 g (1 lb 2 oz) pork bones under cold water, then place in a large saucepan. Peel a 2 cm (¾ inch) piece of fresh ginger and 4 garlic cloves, then cut each in half and add to the pan. Bash 1 lemongrass stem and 2 spring onions (scallions) with the back of a cleaver or mallet, then add them to the pan. Pour in 2 litres (68 fl oz/8 cups) water and bring to the boil. Skim off the impurities from the top of the stock, then reduce the heat and simmer for 2 hours, skimming constantly.

Pour the stock through a fine sieve into a bowl and allow to cool. Once cooled, portion into smaller amounts and refrigerate or freeze until required. The stock will last in the fridge for 3 days, or in the freezer for 3 months.

MS DAEN'S VIETNAMESE/LAO GINGER CHICKEN

SERVES 4 as part of a shared meal

INGREDIENTS

2 tablespoons glutinous rice, soaked in water for 2 hours
2 tablespoons Chicken Stock (page 23)
2 tablespoons vegetable oil
2 garlic cloves, sliced
4 cm (1½ inch) piece of fresh ginger, peeled and julienned
300 g (10½ oz) boneless, skinless chicken breast, finely sliced
1 handful Thai basil leaves
1 handful lemon basil leaves
2 red chillies, sliced
2 tablespoons oyster sauce
pinch of caster (superfine) sugar
coriander (cilantro) sprigs, to garnish
Sticky Rice (page 166), to serve

I'd heard of a family in Vientiane who migrated from Vietnam in the early 1950s and had a restaurant serving the best bowl of 'pho' in town, so naturally I had to check it out. I arrived early for breakfast and met the owner-chef, Ms Daen.

We shared an instant bond. Only later did I learn we were both born in the same refugee camp in Thailand, and even have the same Thai name: Daen.

Her pho was delicious, but it was not a traditional Vietnamese-style pho. Lao cuisine has a strong Vietnamese influence, as many Viet families migrated to Laos during the French occupation and Vietnam War, but the Vietnamese food has changed to accommodate the local palate.

This is Ms Daen's recipe, which she says is a great example of that Vietnamese influence: a Lao version of the Vietnamese ginger chicken.

METHOD

Strain the rice and place in a mortar. Pound with a pestle for 4 minutes, or until crushed. Stir in the chicken stock and set aside.

Add the vegetable oil to a hot wok. Add the garlic and ginger, then sauté over medium-high heat until fragrant.

Add the chicken and stir-fry for 2 minutes over high heat. Now add all the basil and chilli.

Strain the stock mixture from the mortar, discarding the rice. Add to the chicken mixture and stir until combined. Now add the oyster sauce, sugar and a pinch of sea salt and stir-fry for a further minute.

Transfer to a serving platter, garnish with coriander and serve with sticky rice.

LAOS

Picturesque Luang Prabang is nestled in the mountains of central northern Laos, at the confluence of the Mekong and Nam Khan rivers, about 425 kilometres north of Vientiane. A world heritage town, Luang Prabang is as beautiful as it is bountiful; its population of around 400,000 swells each year with tourists travelling from all over the globe to experience its food and culture. As you stroll through the pretty streets, there's a nostalgic old-world charm where old crumbling French villas sit next to golden emerald temples. And while Vientiane may be the nation's capital, its food capital, without a doubt, is Luang Prabang.

Luang Prabang

But before I began my food discovery I had some partying to do. It was the Lao New Year, and water plays a big part in the celebrations, known as Pi Mai. Young people respectfully pour water on their elders, then on monks for blessings of long life and peace. They then spend seven days throwing water at everyone in sight. Sometimes the water is scented with flowers or natural perfumes, but these days people also smear or throw shaving cream, whipped cream, or white powder over each other.

One day while I was drying off, I saw a lady with a street-food cart cooking little sweet coconut cakes, called khao nom kok. I asked her if she could teach me how to make them, and she happily obliged. Chargrilled foods are also popular street fare: chargrilled marinated chicken, beef, buffalo, pork, fish and vegetables are found all through the streets and night markets of Luang Prabang. Another dish I particularly enjoyed were small patties made of finely chopped pork, buffalo, lemongrass, spring onion (scallion), coriander (cilantro) and dill. I asked a local vendor if I could cook these at his stall, and of course he smiled and said, "For sure." The whole family were involved in the business, including Mum, Dad, Auntie, Uncle and young children.

Lao people are just so incredibly friendly and care-free. They are relaxed, smiley, passionate about food – and always willing to teach and share the culture, traditions and cuisine of their proud country.

INGREDIENTS

5 red Asian shallots, roughly chopped
5 lemongrass stems, white part only, chopped
500 g (1 lb 2 oz) minced (ground) buffalo or beef
500 g (1 lb 2 oz) minced (ground) pork
½ teaspoon sea salt
2 teaspoons caster (superfine) sugar
1 teaspoon chilli powder
60 ml (2 fl oz/¼ cup) fish sauce
6 spring onions (scallions), sliced
1 handful chopped dill

STICKY RICE

400 g (14 oz/2 cups) glutinous rice, soaked in cold water overnight

PORK & BUFFALO PATTIES WITH STICKY RICE
MAKES 12 (SERVES 4-6)

The Luang Prabang markets start early in the morning and continue throughout the day and into the night. During the day they are packed with locals buying their daily fresh produce; in the evening, all the foreign travellers venture out to sample traditional Lao cooking – in particular, the barbecue dishes.

Rows and rows of vendors grill everything from whole fish, prawns (shrimp), pork belly, stuffed capsicums (peppers), and these wonderful patties that are chargrilled and eaten with sticky rice. They are extremely tasty and very simple to prepare.

If you can't get your hands on buffalo meat, beef will work fine.

When preparing sticky rice, start a day ahead, as the rice needs overnight soaking.

METHOD

To make the sticky rice, drain and rinse the soaked rice in cold water three times. Pour water into the bottom of your steamer and line the steaming section with muslin (cheesecloth). Place the rinsed rice on the cloth, cover with the lid and set on the stovetop over high heat. Steam for 15 minutes, then flip the rice over. Cook for another 5-15 minutes, or until the rice becomes translucent; take a small bite to check it is soft and chewy. (Sticky rice generally takes about 20-30 minutes of steaming all up.)

Meanwhile, pound the shallot and lemongrass to a paste using a large mortar and pestle. Transfer the paste to a mixing bowl and add the remaining ingredients. Mix together well, then shape into 12 patties, about 6 cm (2¼ inches) across and 2 cm (¾ inch) thick.

Heat a barbecue chargrill or chargrill pan to medium-high. Cook the patties for 3-4 minutes on each side, or until browned and cooked through.

Serve the patties hot, with the sticky rice.

I saw these being grilled at the night markets. When I asked the cook what they were stuffed with, he simply said, "Moo." I thought he was trying to explain the contents by making the sound of a cow – but in Lao, 'moo' means pork, which gave me a bit of a giggle.
I noticed the cooks laid banana leaves on the hot grill, then placed the stuffed capsicums on top to stop them burning. The banana leaf also imparted a great fragrance to the dish – genius!
If you can't find padek, use the pungent Vietnamese fermented anchovy sauce instead, known as 'mam nem'.

INGREDIENTS

3 lemongrass stems, white part only, chopped
4 red Asian shallots, sliced
2 red bird's eye chillies, sliced
500 g (1 lb 2 oz) minced (ground) pork
1 tablespoon caster (superfine) sugar
3 spring onions (scallions), finely sliced
1 handful chopped dill
4 makrut (kaffir lime) leaves, finely sliced
1 tablespoon fish sauce
2 tablespoons padek (Laotian fermented fish sauce; glossary) or mam nem (Vietnamese fermented anchovy sauce; glossary)
4 large or 8 small yellow banana capsicums (peppers)
2 banana leaves, cut into 20 cm x 30 cm (8 inch x 12 inch) rectangles
Sticky Rice (page 166), to serve

CHARGRILLED CAPSICUMS STUFFED WITH PORK & LAO HERBS

SERVES 4 as part of a shared meal

METHOD

Using a large mortar and pestle, pound the lemongrass, shallot and chilli to a rough paste. Now add the pork, sugar and a pinch of sea salt and pound again.

Add the spring onion, dill and makrut leaves and pound well. Now add the fish sauce and half the padek or mam nem and pound again.

Working from the top of each capsicum, use a sharp knife to slice down one side to the stem. Remove the seeds by scraping them out with a small spoon, then discard.

Stuff the capsicums with the pork mixture and set aside.

Heat a barbecue chargrill or chargrill pan to medium-high. Place the banana leaves on top of the grill to stop the capsicums burning. Chargrill the capsicums on top of the banana leaves for 7-8 minutes per side, basting them with the remaining padek or mam nem as they cook.

Serve hot, with sticky rice.

INGREDIENTS

4 hard-boiled eggs
1 bunch watercress, leaves picked
10 iceberg lettuce leaves, torn
1 handful coriander (cilantro) leaves, torn
1 handful celery leaves or mint leaves
1 Lebanese (short) cucumber, sliced
8 cherry tomatoes, quartered
2 teaspoons Fried Garlic (page 82)
2 teaspoons roasted crushed peanuts

DRESSING

2 tablespoons caster (superfine) sugar
1 tablespoon fish sauce
100 ml (3½ fl oz) Garlic Oil (page 82)
2 limes, juiced

LUANG PRABANG SALAD

SERVES 4 as part of a shared meal

If you go to Luang Prabang, be sure to visit the Kuang Xi waterfall. Situated among Hmong Khamu villages and lush green forests only 30 kilometres from town, the 30-metre waterfall cascades down into picturesque turquoise pools, where locals and tourists alike swim.

It was here I noticed a family preparing this classic salad. It is the perfect dish when you are out on a camping trip, or just going for a walk and a swim in the forest, as you don't need any fire. All you need is fresh herbs and vegetables, and some hard-boiled eggs to make a deliciously simple dressing.

METHOD

Peel the hard-boiled eggs, then cut them into quarters. Separate the egg whites and yolks. Place the egg whites in a salad bowl and set aside.

To make the dressing, mash the egg yolks in a mixing bowl. Add the dressing ingredients, along with a pinch of sea salt. Mix together well.

Add the remaining salad ingredients to the egg whites and toss together. Drizzle the dressing over and serve immediately.

When cooking this dish on a gas burner, take extreme care as you may be left with no eyelashes! The beef has Lao whiskey in the marinade and the wok needs to be smoking hot, so you will create high flames as you add the beef. I don't recommend letting children cook this dish.
If you can't get your hands on Lao whiskey, you can use any kind of rice wine that has a high alcohol content.

INGREDIENTS
2 garlic cloves, diced
2 tablespoons Lao whiskey or rice wine with a high alcohol content
1 tablespoon soy sauce
1 tablespoon oyster sauce
1 teaspoon fish sauce
1 teaspoon caster (superfine) sugar
300 g (10 ½ oz) beef fillet, finely sliced
2 tablespoons vegetable oil

SALAD
1 handful coriander (cilantro) leaves, sliced into thirds
3 spring onions (scallions), cut into 3 cm (1¼ inch) lengths
1 handful watercress sprigs, torn
5 butter lettuce leaves, torn
2 tomatoes, finely sliced
2 red Asian shallots, finely sliced
frangipani or marigold petals, to garnish, optional

BEEF WOK-TOSSED IN LAO WHISKEY

SERVES 4 as part of a shared meal

METHOD
Combine the garlic, whiskey, soy sauce, oyster sauce, fish sauce and sugar in a mixing bowl. Mix well to dissolve the sugar. Add the beef and toss until well coated, then cover and leave to marinate for 30 minutes.

Meanwhile, arrange your salad on a serving platter.

Heat a wok or frying pan until smoking hot. Add the vegetable oil and wait until it smokes.

Now add the beef and toss for no longer than 1 minute, taking care as flames will rise. Add a pinch of freshly ground black pepper, then arrange the beef over the salad.

Serve immediately, garnished with frangipani or marigold petals, if desired.

LAOS – LUANG PRABANG

STEAMED FISH IN BANANA LEAVES

SERVES 2

INGREDIENTS

2 tablespoons uncooked glutinous rice
3 lemongrass stems, white part only, sliced
4 small red chillies, sliced
1 red Asian shallot, chopped
1 handful chopped dill
1 handful chopped basil, with flowers if possible
6 spring onions (scallions), sliced
1 teaspoon padek (Laotian fermented fish sauce; glossary) or mam nem (Vietnamese fermented anchovy sauce; glossary)
4 makrut (kaffir lime) leaves, torn
2 x 200 g (7 oz) tilapia or snapper fillets
4 banana leaves, cut into 30 cm (12 inch) squares
Sticky Rice (page 166), to serve

METHOD

Soak the rice for 20 minutes in a small bowl of water. Strain the rice, then tip into a large mortar. Pound with a pestle until it becomes a sticky paste.

Add the lemongrass, chilli and shallot and pound again. Now add the dill, basil and spring onion and pound again.

Add a pinch of sea salt, 1 tablespoon water, the padek or mam nem and the makrut leaves. Cut the fish into 2.5 cm (1 inch) pieces and add them to the mortar too. Mix together with a large spoon.

Soften the banana leaves, either over a gas flame, in a hot frying pan, or by steaming or microwaving them for a few minutes.

Lay two banana leaves on the work surface, at diagonals to one another. Place half the fish mixture in the centre, bring the corners together and join them to form a pyramid. Pin the edges together with toothpicks to secure the filling. Repeat with the remaining ingredients to make a second parcel.

Half-fill a steamer, wok or large saucepan with water and bring to a rapid boil over high heat. Place the parcels in the steamer, flat side down, and steam for 20 minutes.

Serve hot, with sticky rice.

Steaming fish in banana leaves is always a winner. The fish stays moist, while taking on flavour from the leaf itself. It's also a clean, simple, quick and healthy way to cook. The rice is used to combine and attach all the flavours to the fish and, when steamed, contributes a great texture. This is definitely one of my favourite Lao dishes.
In Asia, lemongrass is used when it is young, small and tender. If your lemongrass is old and fibrous, one lemongrass stem will be enough for this recipe.

ALL LAO BOYS SPEND TIME AS NOVICE BUDDHIST MONKS, SHAVING THEIR HEADS AND DONNING BRILLIANT ORANGE ROBES

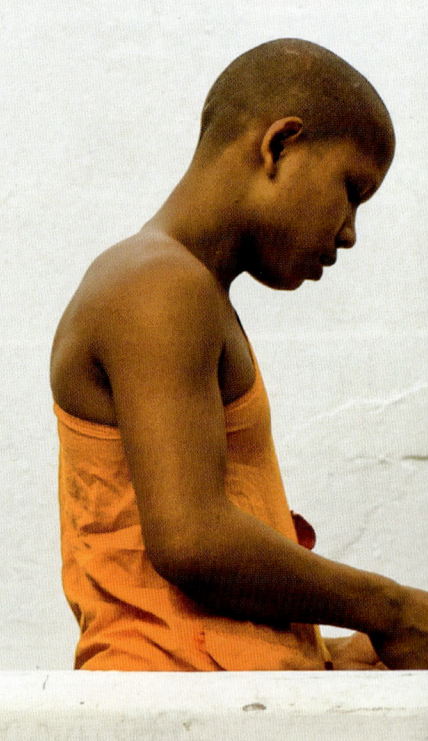

Before heading to Laos, I knew I had to get a one-on-one lesson on how to fold a banana leaf parcel, Lao style. So one of my best friends, Jimmy Vongsuthi, arranged for me to meet up with his mother for a master class. I am so glad I had this lesson, as so many Lao dishes call for intricate banana leaf folding – but don't worry, this recipe calls for one of the easier folds!

When purchasing banana leaves from your Asian market, don't buy the ones flown in from Thailand. Go for the fresher local ones, which should be vibrant green in colour.

INGREDIENTS

500 g (1 lb 2 oz) glutinous rice, soaked in water overnight
400 ml (14 fl oz) coconut milk
½ teaspoon sea salt
200 g (7 oz) caster (superfine) sugar
1 tablespoon vegetable oil
4 large banana leaves, cut into 20 cm x 30 cm (8 inch x 12 inch) rectangles
4 ripe bananas, peeled and cut in half lengthways, then crossways

STEAMED STICKY RICE CAKES WITH BANANA

MAKES 16

METHOD

Strain the rice and place it in a hot wok or saucepan. Stir in the coconut milk, salt and sugar. Bring to a simmer and cook for 4-6 minutes, or until the coconut milk has been absorbed and the rice is thick and sticky. Stir in the oil, then transfer the mixture to a tray and cool for 5-10 minutes.

Soften the banana leaves, either over a gas flame, in a hot frying pan, or by steaming or microwaving them for a few minutes. Lay a banana leaf on the work surface. Place one heaped tablespoon of the cooled rice in the centre of the leaf. Next add a single piece of banana, followed by ½ tablespoon rice on top of the banana – the banana should be sandwiched between the rice. Now fold the sides of the leaves over, as you would a parcel.

Repeat with the remaining rice, banana and banana leaves. If you have softened the leaves properly, you won't need to use anything extra to secure the parcels.

Half-fill a large steamer, wok or saucepan with water and bring to a rapid boil over high heat. Place the parcels in your steamer basket, seam side down, and set it over the pan of water. Steam for 30 minutes.

Enjoy the sticky rice cakes hot.

LAOS-LUANG PRABANG

SWEET COCONUT CAKES

MAKES 25-35 (SERVES 4-6 as a snack)

INGREDIENTS
500 ml (17 fl oz/2 cups) coconut milk
375 g (13 oz) rice flour
125 g (4 oz) caster (superfine) sugar
vegetable oil, for brushing

These sweet little delights are sold as a street-food snack all through Laos. They are very addictive, so you'll find yourself having a dozen all to yourself.

I came across a lady making these cakes on a bicycle cart during the busy New Year's festival. She kindly agreed to teach me, so we prepared 10 litres (about 20 pints) of batter and sold out within the hour. Each portion had six cakes and we sold them for $1, in an intricate hand-folded banana leaf cup – bargain!

You can buy special pans designed for these cakes from Asian suppliers. Ask for 'khao nom kok' (Thai/Laos) pans, or 'banh khot' (Vietnamese) pans. You can also use a Dutch pancake pan.

METHOD

Place the coconut milk, rice flour and sugar in a mixing bowl. Add a pinch of sea salt and 500 ml (17 fl oz/2 cups) water and whisk until completely smooth.

Heat a khao nom kok pan or a Dutch pancake pan (poffertjes pan) to medium. Brush each mould or hole with vegetable oil.

Before proceeding, make sure the pan is hot, or the cakes will be difficult to remove. Pour the batter into each mould, close the lid and cook for 4-5 minutes, or until the cakes are browned and crisp, but still moist in the centre.

Using an oiled stainless steel Chinese soup spoon or a teaspoon, remove the cakes from the pan.

Cook the remaining batter in the same way. Serve hot.

LAOS

Laos is not usually mentioned in the same sentence as 'island', as the Mekong is the nation's only major body of water. However, the area known as Si Phan Don does, in fact, have islands – several thousand of them actually.

On its way down to Cambodia, the Mekong spills across and around a giant expanse of rocks, rapids and islands. Like the rest of Laos, this area is quiet, quaint, and a great place to relax. And it has some of the craziest fish and insect dishes in the country!

4000 Islands

The drive from Luang Prabang was long and hot, hitting 41 degrees Celsius. We had to stop the bus more than a dozen times to buy ice-blocks to cool us down; everyone was hot and bothered. This all changed when we reached the river and discovered the beauty of this area. There were butterflies everywhere, birds chirping, the trees were tall, lush and plentiful, and clear emerald-green waters fanned out across many small islands. It was the most picturesque part of the Mekong that I had seen so far.

We hopped on a boat to Don Khone island, to Lipi waterfalls, which flow into rough rapids. We spent time with local fishermen, who were catching small river fish to make padek – Lao's pungent fish sauce. At this time of year, the fish swim upstream to spawn, so the local fishermen attach bamboo traps to the rocks to catch them during mid-flight. Mav, our cameraman, wanted to get a close-up shot of the little fish jumping out of the water against the strong rapids. But he slipped and lost his little Go Pro camera. After an hour of searching, the fishermen retrieved the camera, which was still working thanks to its waterproof housing. Hilariously, it did take some incredible underwater footage of various freshwater fish!

With all the fish we caught that day, a fishing family showed me a typical dish that they would cook after a day's fishing in the cold water. They gathered sticks and built a fire right on the water's edge, then simmered a broth made from fish bones, garlic, shallots, young coconut water, tamarind, lemongrass, chilli and padek for 20 minutes. The family then gathered around the fire and hotpot, threading fresh fish fillets and vegetables onto a bamboo skewer, then each person cooked their own skewer by dunking it into the simmering hotpot and taking it out when the food was cooked. I just loved this way of cooking and eating. It brought the whole family together after a long, hard day's work, and made cooking communal and lots of fun.

I said my goodbyes, then continued to a small village in search of a special insect dish I'd heard so much about ...

RIVER FISH STEAM BOAT

SERVES 4

INGREDIENTS

1 tablespoon vegetable oil
1 small onion, cut into wedges
2 garlic cloves, finely sliced
2 red Asian shallots, finely sliced
1 cm (½ inch) piece of fresh ginger, peeled and finely sliced
1 tablespoon tamarind pulp (with the seeds; not tamarind purée)
2 teaspoons chilli flakes
500 g (1 lb 2 oz) whole white-fleshed fish, such as snapper, cut into fillets and finely sliced, reserving the bones for the broth
1 tablespoon unsalted roasted peanuts
1 tablespoon caster (superfine) sugar
1 tablespoon fish sauce
1 tablespoon soy sauce
1 litre (34 fl oz/4 cups) young coconut juice (glossary)
1 lemongrass stem, bruised
juice of 1 lime
2 eggs, beaten
½ teaspoon freshly ground black pepper
16 butter lettuce leaves
7 Chinese cabbage leaves, finely sliced
1 large handful mint leaves
4 spring onions (scallions), cut into 3 cm (1¼ inch) lengths
1 large handful coriander (cilantro), roughly chopped
1 large handful water spinach, torn into 3 cm (1¼ inch) lengths

METHOD

Start by making the broth. Add the vegetable oil to a hot wok, then sauté the onion, garlic, shallot and ginger until browned. Stir in the tamarind pulp and chilli flakes. Now add the reserved fish bones and toss to coat them well.

Add the peanuts, sugar, fish sauce, soy sauce, coconut juice, lemongrass, lime juice, half the beaten egg and a pinch of sea salt. Simmer for 15 minutes.

On a separate plate, mix the sliced fish fillets with the pepper and the remaining egg.

Now take one lettuce leaf and place a little cabbage, mint, spring onion, coriander, water spinach and a few fish slices on top. Wrap the lettuce up around the filling, then secure the ends with a bamboo skewer.

Repeat with the remaining ingredients, securing each parcel with a bamboo skewer.

Cook the fish parcels in the simmering broth for 1 minute, then enjoy straight away.

I spent the day with a local family who catch small freshwater fish to make padek, the Lao fish sauce. Boys young and old would spend hours in the freezing waters, throwing their nets out, then diving on top to trap the fish. They would place the fish in large buckets for the girls, as young as six, to debone and fillet! When they finished, the family would build a fire right on the water's edge and cook up this steamboat.
This is such a wonderful dish as it brings family and friends together. Everyone has great fun preparing and cooking their own. When buying young coconut juice, try to source juice from fresh green coconuts – the tinned juice has too much added sugar.

At a small village not far from Don Khone, I was given a long bamboo pole with a basket tied to one end. I was told to raise the basket up under a tree branch, beneath an ants' nest, and shake vigorously. Hundreds of ants fell into the basket, but many dozens landed on my head and down my shirt — I was bitten everywhere! It was the first time I could honestly say I had 'ants in my pants'! After the stinging subsided, I scooped the red ants and their larvae into a bucket of cold water. They were washed, strained, then tossed into this salad. As the ants dried off, they came back to life and tried to crawl out of the salad bowl. I was told I had to eat them alive. One bit the inside of my mouth as I took a bite — but the eggs were a textural delight, popping as I bit into them. This salad was one of the most exciting and craziest dishes that I've ever made and eaten in South-East Asia. Loved it!

INGREDIENTS

3 tablespoons red ant eggs
2 spring onions (scallions), finely sliced
3 red Asian shallots, finely sliced
2 lemongrass stems, white part only, finely sliced
1 small handful coriander (cilantro), sliced
10 mint leaves, sliced
10 Vietnamese mint leaves, sliced
3 saw-tooth coriander (cilantro) leaves (glossary), sliced
1 teaspoon padek (Laotian fermented fish sauce; glossary)
½ teaspoon fish sauce
½ teaspoon chilli flakes
1 teaspoon Toasted Rice Powder (see Note)
juice of 1 lime
10 small Chinese cabbage leaves

RED ANT EGG SALAD

SERVES 4 as part of a shared meal

METHOD

Combine all the ingredients, except the cabbage leaves, in a mixing bowl. Toss together well, then transfer to a serving platter.

Serve the cabbage leaves with the salad, using them as a 'spoon' to eat the salad with.

NOTE

Lao people use toasted rice powder in dishes such as laap (page 161), and for dipping unripe fruit in, such as pomelo, green mango, tamarind and guava. Heat a frying pan or wok over medium heat and dry-roast 100 g (3½ oz/½ cup) uncooked glutinous rice for 8–10 minutes, until lightly browned, tossing occasionally. (For a smokier flavour, allow the rice to turn a deeper shade of brown; to make your rice powder more perfumed, you can also dry-roast the rice with chilli, lemongrass and makrut (kaffir lime leaves).) Remove from the heat and allow to cool, then pound to a powder using a large mortar and pestle. It is best used fresh, but can be stored in an airtight container in a cool, dark place for several weeks.

CHAPTER 5

Cambodia

SIEM REAP TO KAMPOT

Cambodia
SIEM REAP TO KAMPOT

The people of Cambodia seem to share a real closeness – a sense of connection I have not seen in any other country. Perhaps it's because everyone here has a story to tell of losing family during the Pol Pot regime. When people told me their stories of food in Cambodia, it always led back to a time of trauma and genocide. But then the conversation would slip back even further in time, and people would smile and reminisce about their childhood, of a grandmother's recipe, or a special dish that somebody still knows the recipe for.

I loved the food in this country – and I love that by piecing together fragments of the collective memory, people are reclaiming and revitalising the country's national cuisine.

My travels in Cambodia began in Siem Reap. The temples and estates of Angkor Wat are fascinating and beautiful; the township is charming, with its stunning French colonial buildings, and cute alleyways and back streets that open out to wider boulevards. The canals that meander through the city are being slowly restored, becoming cleaner and more appealing.

As Cambodia's main tourist destination, the city is far more developed than other areas of the country. There was a buzz in Siem Reap, and the changes seemed to be made in good faith and in the hope of the nation prospering.

Culture, history, rural farming and inner-city cool sit side by side in Siem Reap, and it was here that I experienced some of the most memorable Khmer cuisine.

Further south, I arrived in the capital, Phnom Penh. It instantly felt more like a big city that is forging ahead as the country's business centre. This is where you find the true Cambodia: within minutes of arriving you are confronted with old and new, poor and rich, harshness and kindness, honesty and corruption.

The food scene reflected this dichotomy, with the most basic kerbside meals for workers on one hand, in stark contrast to the grand and exquisite surrounds of high-end restaurants serving traditional cuisine, with all the bells and whistles.

I finished my Khmer food trail by the sea, at Kampot and Kep, renowned for green peppercorns, sweet crab and tender squid. The seafood catches are getting smaller every year, but at the same time tourism is growing.

Like the rest of Cambodia, the region is in transition. I hope great things are yet to come for the Khmer people. If anyone deserves a time of peace and prosperity, it is the people of Cambodia.

FOR CENTURIES, THE HALLS AND TEMPLES OF ANGKOR HAVE BEEN HOME TO PRAYER AND WORSHIP. THEY STILL INSPIRE RELIGIOUS DEVOTION AND PILGRIMS FROM AFAR

CAMBODIA

Siem Reap, in north-west Cambodia, is the country's fastest growing city and serves as a charming gateway to the world-famous Angkor temples. Its name, which translates as 'the flat defeat of Siam', refers to the centuries-old conflict between the Thai and Khmer people.

Thanks to Angkor Wat, Siem Reap has become a major tourist hub, with modern hotels, restaurants and bars. But despite all the international influences, the people have managed to preserve much of the town's image, culture and traditions.

Siem Reap

When I arrived in Siem Reap, I was ready to dive in head-first to discover the history of ancient Khmer food. My first port of call was the Sugar Palm restaurant, where I met the lovely cook, Khetana. Like so many Khmer people, she lived through the genocide that swept her country, emerging as a leader in the food and culture scene of the new Cambodia. Khetana explained that Khmer food has much in common with that of its neighbours, especially Vietnam and Thailand. The subtle flavours and balance of ingredients reflect the core traits of Vietnamese cuisine.

We stopped at a roadside stall, where I was shown how to make palm sugar. Skilled climbers scale palm trees, then wedge the palm nuts between two sticks and extract the sweet juice from the nut. This juice is slowly cooked in large woks over low heat until the juice caramelises into a thick, sweet, golden syrup. After two hours of cooking and stirring, palm sugar is created. Locals use the palm sugar in its syrup form, but it is cooked for longer and formed into solid blocks for export.

The next day I found a family willing to teach me how to make my childhood favourite, lap cheong. I'd bought some fatty pork sausages in the Psa Leu market, so I was ready to have a go. The family had been making lap cheong for three generations. Their secret sat in blue plastic drums in the basement of their house. The drums were filled with Chinese rice wine that had been infused with star anise and cassia bark for at least six months. This prized liquid was the marinade for the pork, and gave the sausages a deep flavour and aroma, and a lovely red colour.

At Kompong Phluk I saw a most unusual floating fishing village: it was dry season, so the village was floating on a dry, dusty river bed! Quite a contrast to when the rains come. During the dry period, people spend their days sifting through cockles, catching shrimp and drying them on the river bed. Kids play cards or other games; many seem to get an education from life, rather than through schoolbooks. It was here I learnt how to dry shrimp. And came face to face with the hard lives most Khmer endure.

INGREDIENTS

1 large or 2 small green mangoes, peeled and finely shredded
3 tablespoons dried shrimp (glossary), soaked in water for 20 minutes
100 g (3½ oz) hot smoked trout, shredded
1 handful mixed mint, Vietnamese mint and Thai basil leaves
2 red Asian shallots, finely sliced
2 tablespoons roasted crushed unsalted peanuts
½ teaspoon Garlic Oil (see Note, page 82)
1 bird's eye chilli, sliced

DRESSING

1 tablespoon fish sauce
1 tablespoon white sugar
60 ml (2 fl oz/¼ cup) hot water

GREEN MANGO & DRIED SHRIMP SALAD

SERVES 4 as part of a shared meal

METHOD

Combine the dressing ingredients in a mixing bowl and stir until the sugar has dissolved.

Place the mango, dried shrimp, trout, mint and shallot in a salad bowl. Add 60 ml (2 fl oz/¼ cup) of the dressing and mix well.

Garnish with the peanuts and chilli and drizzle with the garlic oil. Serve the remaining dressing on the side for drizzling.

A few hours south-east of Siem Reap, I arrived at a floating village called Kompong Phluk. Surreally, it was dry season and there was no water at all! This meant local shrimp fishermen had to travel far to go about their daily work. Their technique was amazing to watch. They would float in the water with a large leafy branch. As the shrimp made their way downstream, they would cling to the branch and under the leaves for safety. The men would slowly raise the branch, place a bamboo basket underneath and shake the branch until all the shrimp fell into the basket below. The shrimp are steamed, peeled, salted and dried, then sold to big city markets. Now that I've seen how much time and work goes into preparing dried shrimp, I'll never complain about the price again. The saltiness of dried shrimp works wonderfully with the sour-sweet flavours of green mango. When buying green mango, choose a firm one. If it is soft, it is too ripe for this salad.

KHMER FISH SALAD

SERVES 4 as part of a shared meal

INGREDIENTS

80 g (3 oz) snake head fish or snapper fillet, finely sliced
25 g (1 oz/½ cup) finely shredded white cabbage
25 g (1 oz/½ cup) finely shredded purple cabbage
25 g (1 oz/½ cup) finely shredded iceberg lettuce
½ Lebanese (short) cucumber, finely sliced
80 g (3 oz/½ cup) finely sliced green capsicum (pepper)
½ carrot, finely shredded
2 red Asian shallots, finely sliced
2 snake (yard-long) beans, very finely sliced
1 small handful bean sprouts
1 small handful mint leaves
1 small handful Vietnamese mint leaves
1 small handful Thai basil leaves
2 teaspoons sugar
1 teaspoon fish sauce

LIME MARINADE

1 teaspoon Coriander Paste (see Note)
pinch of sliced lemongrass, white part only
125 ml (4 fl oz/½ cup) lime juice

TO GARNISH

roasted crushed unsalted peanuts
sliced red chillies

The fish in this salad is citrus-cured. It is 'cold cooked' in the sense that it is the acid in the lime that actually 'cooks' the fish. This method of cooking is brilliant as it is quick, healthy and doesn't require any heat. I'd planned on making this dish at Angkor Wat, but officials changed their minds at the last minute. So, being such a simple and clean dish to prepare, I took all the ingredients on a tuk-tuk and made it while going on a city tour of Siem Reap! We could only fit three in the tuk-tuk. It was a squashed, bumpy and dangerous ride, but we did have loads of fun.

METHOD

Combine the lime marinade ingredients in a mixing bowl with a pinch of sea salt. Stir until the salt has dissolved.

Now add the fish and leave to cure for 10 minutes. Squeeze all the lime marinade out of the fish and reserve.

Combine all the vegetables, bean sprouts and herbs in a large salad bowl.

Add the fish to the salad, along with the sugar, fish sauce and 60 ml (2 fl oz/¼ cup) of the reserved lime marinade.

Mix well, garnish with peanuts and chilli and serve.

NOTE

To make the coriander paste, combine 1 tablespoon chopped red Asian shallots in a mortar and pestle or small food processor with 1 tablespoon chopped garlic, 2 teaspoons chopped fresh galangal and 1 small handful chopped coriander (cilantro). Pound or process until a paste forms. Transfer to a screw-top jar and store in the refrigerator. The mixture will keep for up to 4 days.

INGREDIENTS

50 g (2 oz/¼ cup) glutinous rice
½ teaspoon sea salt
625 ml (21 fl oz/2½ cups) coconut milk
4 fresh sugar palm fruits (glossary), or 200 g (7 oz) tinned sugar palm fruit, drained and sliced
3 tablespoons liquid palm sugar (glossary), or shaved palm sugar (jaggery)
80 ml (2½ fl oz/⅓ cup) coconut cream

SUGAR PALM WITH COCONUT MILK
SERVES 4

The palmyra palm tree is Cambodia's national tree, and it is the sweet sap of its sugar palm fruit that is used to make the much-loved palm sugar or jaggery.
Sugar palm fruit is also known as ice-apple. The flesh is clear and the texture is unique, almost jelly-like.
This sweet pudding is my new favourite South-East Asian dessert, as it has the sugar palm fruit, its juice and also palm sugar. If you can't find fresh sugar palm fruit, use the tinned form, labelled as sugar palm seeds or pulp. Wash it before using, as it may be soaked in overly sweet sugar syrup.

METHOD

Soak the rice in water for 20 minutes, then strain.

Add the rice to a saucepan, along with the salt and half the coconut milk. Bring to the boil, then reduce the heat and simmer for 5 minutes, stirring occasionally, until the rice softens.

Meanwhile, if using fresh sugar palm fruit, peel the fruit and remove the stones, working over a bowl to catch the juices. Finely slice the fruit, then set the juice aside.

Add the sugar palm fruit and remaining coconut milk to the rice. Stir, then cook for a further 5 minutes, or until the rice becomes translucent.

Now stir in the palm sugar and cook for a further 2 minutes.

Divide the mixture among four bowls. Drizzle each with a tablespoon of the coconut cream and serve warm.

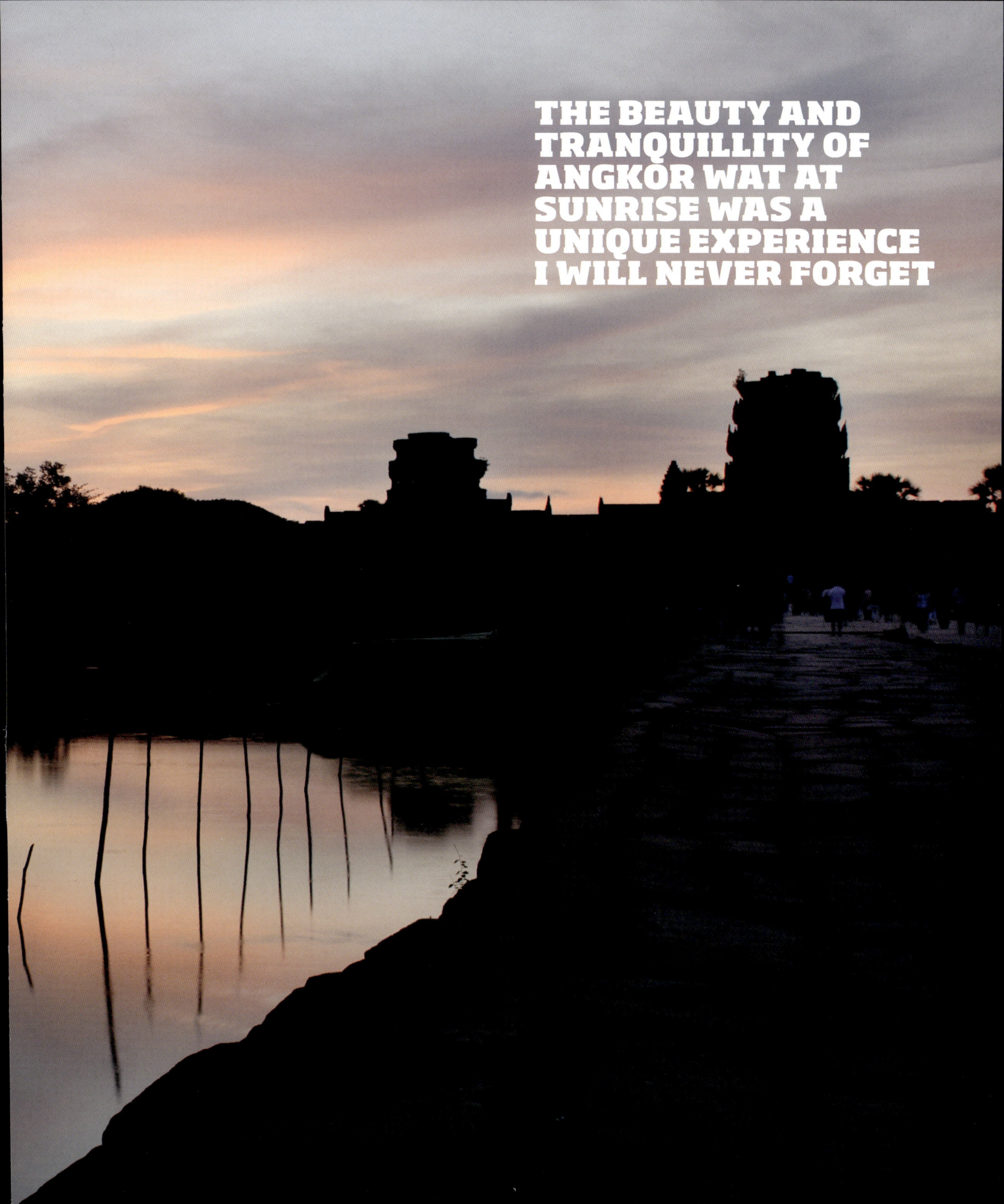

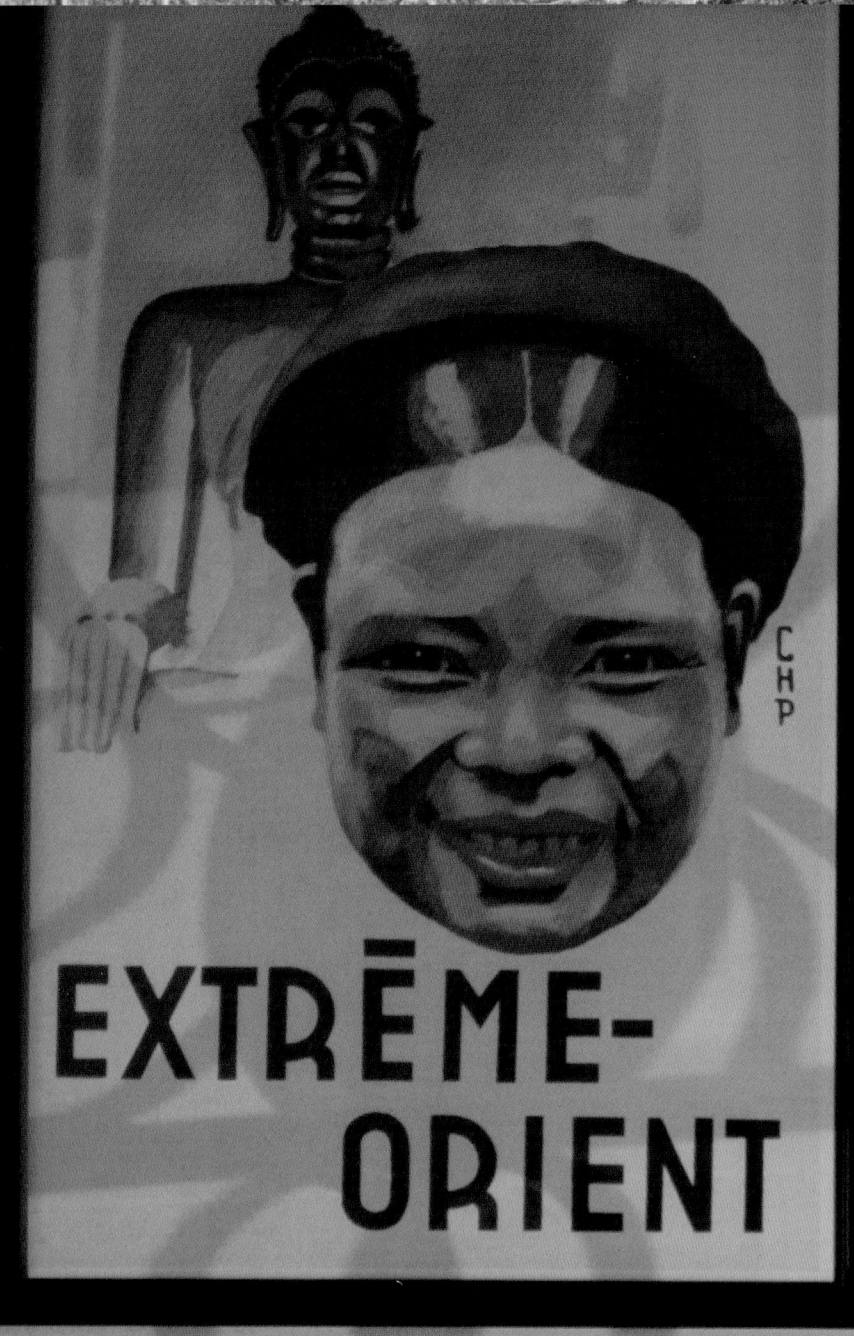

CAMBODIA

Once known as the 'Pearl of Asia', Phnom Penh was considered one of the loveliest French-built cities in Indochina. It has been the nation's capital since the French colonised Cambodia. Located on the banks of the mighty Mekong, it is the country's largest city, and its economic, political and industrial heart.

Phnom Penh

At a rest stop at Kampong Cham, on the way to Phnom Penh, I noticed ladies selling trays of deep-fried insects as snacks. Only when I walked closer did I realise the snacks were in fact hundreds of deep-fried tarantulas! I'm not a big fan of spiders, and as I was steeling myself to pop one in my mouth, a local man tried to put two hairy live tarantulas on my chest and shoulder. After having the live tarantulas on my chest, it was easier to eat the fried ones! They didn't taste too bad: the legs and head were crunchy, but the body was a bit gooey, oozing a liquid resembling creamy peanut butter. They explained that during the Khmer Rouge rule, there was so little food, people ate tarantulas to survive.

I wanted to learn how they hunt and catch tarantulas, so we drove 15 minutes out of town to an open field where we were introduced to a lady known as the 'spider whisperer'. She took us to some tarantula burrows, where she got down on her knees, put her mouth against the opening of a hole and began to hum and sing into the burrow. Her voice's vibrations lured the spider out. As the spider revealed its head, she told me to dig the spider out of its burrow. She picked up the spider with her bare hands, then passed it to her seven-year-old daughter to hold onto, while she set off to catch some more. It was quite magical to see.

In Phnom Penh, I was hit with the heavy contrast between the old and new Cambodia. Gorgeous old colonial buildings and the golden Royal Palace sit alongside high-rise city buildings, five-star hotels and fine restaurants.

In Phnom Penh, one particular chef has been working hard for decades to bring back ancient Khmer cuisine. I met Luu Meng for lunch at Malis, one of his many restaurants. Meng developed his passion for cooking from his grandmother, who had a restaurant in Phnom Penh. He said Cambodian cuisine was well established around 1965, but creativity stopped because of the war. After studying cooking in Thailand, Malaysia, Singapore and Vietnam, he returned to Cambodia to revitalise traditional Khmer food. Meng is a living example of the people's humble, enduring resilience.

On Friday and Saturday evenings, the grounds outside the Royal Palace turn into street-food heaven. Vendors sell all the local favourites: steamed duck embryo egg, snails tossed with lemongrass and chilli, fish soup with noodles, rice paper rolls, chargrilled pork sausage, dried squid, and of course cold beer to wash it all down.

Locals hire bamboo mats and sit on the ground outside the palace enjoying the goods on offer. To see the royal family on one side of the wall, and the other side lined with street food and locals, is such a buzz. When pan-frying these prawn cakes, make them as flat and thin as you can before transferring them to the deep-frying oil.

INGREDIENTS
125 g (4 oz/1 cup) tempura flour (glossary)
200 g (7 oz) raw prawn (shrimp) meat, finely chopped
vegetable oil, for deep-frying

LIME DIPPING SAUCE
250 ml (8½ fl oz/1 cup) lime juice
1 teaspoon freshly ground black pepper
1 teaspoon sea salt

PRAWN CAKES
MAKES 12 (SERVES 4 as part of a shared meal)

METHOD
Combine the lime dipping sauce ingredients in a bowl and stir until the salt has dissolved. Set aside.

In a mixing bowl, whisk the flour with 185 ml (6½ fl oz/¾ cup) water to form a smooth batter. Add the prawn meat and mix again.

Heat 80 ml (2½ fl oz/⅓ cup) vegetable oil in a large frying pan over medium heat. In a wok, also heat enough vegetable oil for deep-frying to 180°C (350°F), or until a cube of bread dropped into the oil browns in 15 seconds.

For each prawn cake, add 2 tablespoons of the prawn mixture to the frying pan; as soon as the mixture hits the pan, flatten each cake, using the spoon or a spatula, to about 2.5 mm (⅛ inch). Fry for 1 minute, then transfer to the wok and deep-fry for 5 minutes on each side. Drain on paper towels.

Serve warm, with the lime dipping sauce.

INGREDIENTS

450 g (1 lb) water spinach
2 tablespoons vegetable oil
4 garlic cloves, smashed
2 tablespoons oyster sauce
2 tablespoons fermented soya beans (glossary)
2 teaspoons liquid palm sugar (glossary), or shaved palm sugar (jaggery)
1 long red chilli, finely sliced

WATER SPINACH WITH FERMENTED SOYA BEANS

SERVES 4 as part of a shared meal

METHOD

Wash the spinach well. Tear the spinach into 4 cm (1½ inch) lengths, discarding any tough thick stems towards the bottom.

Add the vegetable oil to a hot wok and sauté the garlic over high heat until slightly browned.

Add the spinach and toss for 1 minute. Now add the oyster sauce, soya beans and palm sugar and toss for a further minute.

Transfer to a serving plate, garnish with the chilli and serve.

I woke at 4am to get to a water spinach village in time for the morning harvest. The whole village gets involved: men, women and children. Their working day begins as the sun rises; they step out of their wooden stilt houses and straight onto narrow canoes and row to the middle of the fields, where they pull and chop the spinach out of the water. There were water spinach fields as far as the eye could see, an endless carpet of breathtaking greenery, dotted with canoes and conical hats.

Water spinach is my absolute favourite green vegetable. It is succulent yet crisp, and so versatile. Cook it in soups, toss it through salads and noodles, or stir-fry it with other ingredients. It is also known as kangkong, Chinese spinach, swamp cabbage or morning glory.

When buying fermented soya beans, go for the brown ones sold in glass jars.

PAN-FRIED PRAWNS WITH PRAHOK RICE

SERVES 4

INGREDIENTS

250 g (9 oz/1¼ cups) jasmine rice
8 raw jumbo king prawns (shrimp) or scampi, about 400 g (14 oz) in total
1 tablespoon oyster sauce
½ teaspoon freshly ground black pepper
vegetable oil, for pan-frying
1 sprig of green kampot pepper, or 12 fresh green kampot peppercorns (glossary), or at a pinch the ones sold in brine
95 g (3½ oz/½ cup) diced ripe mango
1 tablespoon shaved palm sugar (jaggery)
1 egg, beaten
Pickled Vegetables (page 212), to serve

SPICE PASTE

1 tablespoon vegetable oil
2 makrut (kaffir lime) leaves, finely sliced
2 teaspoons Cambodian Chilli Paste (see Note, page 218)
1 teaspoon Kroeung Paste (see Note, page 212)
1 garlic clove, finely chopped
2 red Asian shallots, finely chopped
250 ml (8½ fl oz/1 cup) coconut cream
1 teaspoon prahok (Cambodian fermented fish paste) or mam ruoc (Vietnamese fermented shrimp paste; glossary)

I spent hours with chef Luu Meng, owner of the Malis restaurant in Phnom Penh, eating and chatting about Khmer cuisine and how it almost disappeared under Pol Pot's Communist regime. Luu was so passionate about his country, culture and cuisine, giving a real insight into the flavours of Khmer cooking. This recipe is actually best with leftover cold rice, so cook it ahead if you have time. Prahok is sold in glass jars at Asian stores.

METHOD

Put the rice in a saucepan with 450 ml (15 fl oz) water and bring to a simmer. Cover and cook over medium-low heat for 16 minutes, or until the water is absorbed. Remove from the heat and stand, covered, for 10 minutes. Allow to cool.

Peel and devein the prawns, leaving the tail and head intact. Rub the prawns with the oyster sauce, pepper and a pinch of sea salt. Set aside.

To make the spice paste, add the vegetable oil to a hot frying pan. Add the makrut leaves, chilli paste, kroeung paste, garlic and shallot and sauté over medium heat until fragrant. Add half the coconut cream, stirring until red and orange colours develop. Now add the remaining coconut cream and stir again for a further minute. Add the prahok, stir, then transfer to a bowl and set aside.

Wipe the pan clean and place back over medium heat. When the pan is hot, add another tablespoon of vegetable oil, the kampot pepper sprig or peppercorns, the mango and palm sugar. Stir until the mango starts to caramelise. Remove the mixture from the pan, wipe the pan clean and add a little more oil to it.

Add the prawns. Scoop out the orange butter inside the prawn heads (called the 'tomalley'), by angling the heads back from the bodies and scraping out the goo, into the pan. Add the beaten egg, mixing everything together.

Return the mango to the pan, along with the steamed rice and cooked spice paste. Stir-fry for 2 minutes, then remove from the heat.

Scoop the fried rice onto a plate; pick out the prawns and arrange them over the rice. Serve with pickled vegetables.

KHMER BEEF SKEWERS

MAKES 8 skewers (SERVES 4)

INGREDIENTS
2 tablespoons fish sauce
1 tablespoon liquid palm sugar (glossary), or shaved palm sugar (jaggery)
2 tablespoons Annatto Oil (see Note, page 241)
4 tablespoons Kreoung Paste (see Note)
500 g (1 lb 2 oz) beef brisket, finely sliced
4 Vietnamese baguettes

PICKLED VEGETABLES
70 ml (2¼ fl oz) fish sauce
70 ml (2¼ fl oz) white vinegar
125 g (4 oz) sugar
500 g (1 lb 2 oz) green papaya, peeled and shredded
½ carrot, peeled and shredded
2 long red chillies, finely sliced

METHOD
Make the pickled vegetables a day ahead. Combine the fish sauce, vinegar, sugar and 250 ml (8½ fl oz/1 cup) water in a saucepan and bring to the boil. Remove from the heat and allow to cool to room temperature. Transfer the mixture to an airtight container and add the papaya, carrot and chilli. Mix well, seal and leave to pickle overnight, or for 24 hours.

The beef can also be marinated well ahead. Combine the fish sauce, palm sugar, annatto oil and kreoung paste in a mixing bowl with a pinch of sea salt. Stir until the salt has dissolved, then add the beef and mix until well coated. Cover and leave to marinate in the refrigerator for up to 24 hours, but at least 2 hours.

When you're nearly ready to cook, soak eight bamboo skewers in cold water for 30 minutes.

Heat a barbecue chargrill or chargrill pan to medium. Thread the beef onto the skewers and chargrill for 2–3 minutes on each side, or until cooked to your liking.

Slice the baguettes lengthways halfway through, creating a pocket. Fill each one with some pickled vegetables and two beef skewers. Pull the skewers out of the rolls and serve.

NOTE
Kroeung paste is an essential base for many Cambodian dishes. Use a large mortar and pestle or a food processor to pound or process the following to a smooth paste: 3 tablespoons peeled, sliced fresh galangal; 3 tablespoons peeled, sliced fresh turmeric; 6 sliced garlic cloves; 2 finely sliced lemongrass stems, white part only; 2 sliced red Asian shallots; 10 finely shredded makrut (kaffir lime) leaves; 6 sliced bird's eye chillies; 2 sliced long red chillies; 1 teaspoon black peppercorns; 1 teaspoon sea salt; 1 teaspoon shrimp paste and 60 ml (2 fl oz/¼ cup) vegetable oil. You can refrigerate the spice paste in a clean screw-top jar for up to 2 weeks.

Like Laos and Vietnam, Cambodia was colonised by the French. Many French buildings still stand tall today and the food has strong French influences. In the late afternoon, street-food stalls appear, chargrilling these beef skewers, served in a warm, crisp baguette with pickled vegetables.

Chef Sakal introduced me to this local favourite. His whole family were killed during the Khmer Rouge regime, but Sakal luckily fled to France, where he learnt the culinary arts from the age of sixteen. He says this dish resembles himself: French on the outside, but a true Cambodian inside. You'll only need half the pickled vegetables on the baguettes, so use the remainder as an accompaniment to other Cambodian meals.

CAMBODIA

From the early 1900s to the 1960s, Kep was a thriving resort town for the French and Cambodian elite. However, many of its mansions and villas were destroyed during the Khmer Rouge years. Some say locals, in desperate need of money and food, stripped down their own buildings, exchanging all the valuable bits in nearby Vietnam for food. Today the town is known for its seafood, especially blue swimmer crab, yet some of its former splendour remains.

Kep & Kampot

We arrive in Kep at lunchtime. The wide sidewalks along the oceanfront are lined with colourful hammocks swinging under wooden huts. Locals drive from all over Cambodia with their friends and family, hire a hut and devour the fresh seafood on offer. Each hut has a table that seats about twelve people cross-legged. Guitars come out, along with durian, lychees, sing-alongs, beer and lots of crab bought from the early-morning Kep crab market.

Families pay about $20 to hire a hut for an afternoon, and an extra $10 to have their freshly purchased seafood cooked up for them. It's clearly a good business to be in, and because we were foreigners and had a big camera, they charged us double!

The town of Kampot, a mere 20 kilometres away, is famous for its fresh green peppercorns, renowned as one of the finest peppers in the world. The proximity of the sea and a nearby mountain chain give Kampot a unique climate, with heavy and regular rainfall.

At the end of the 19th century, Kampot province experienced a 'pepper fever' with the arrival of French colonists, who intensified the pepper production, churning out up to 8000 tonnes a year.

The pepper industry declined completely during the Khmer Rouge years, but farmers afterwards returned to their land and the pepper industry made a comeback. Today it is one of the biggest exporters of quality pepper in the world.

Now there is pepper, and there is Kampot pepper, which is strong, spicy, but also delicate, sweet, floral and aromatic. I used the pepper in everything I cooked there: tamarind crab with kampot pepper; baby squid wok-tossed with kampot pepper, and even kampot pepper ice cream!

Through all the amazing and inspirational people I met in Cambodia, I truly feel like I left with a real understanding of the food and culture, and I really look forward to seeing how Khmer cuisine develops in the coming years.

KAMPOT COLD NOODLES

SERVES 4 as part of a shared meal

INGREDIENTS
2 tablespoons dried shrimp (glossary)
100 g (3½ oz) vermicelli noodles
3 iceberg lettuce leaves, finely shredded
100 g (3½ oz) bean sprouts
1 Lebanese (short) cucumber, cut into thin batons
1 handful mixed mint, Vietnamese mint and basil leaves
2 tablespoons roasted crushed unsalted peanuts

SWEET FISH SAUCE DRESSING
4 garlic cloves, chopped
1 small red chilli, chopped
2 tablespoons sugar
2 tablespoons fish sauce
125 ml (4 fl oz/½ cup) lime juice

THICKENED COCONUT DRESSING
2 teaspoons vegetable oil
½ spring onion (scallion), finely sliced
125 ml (4 fl oz/½ cup) coconut cream
½ teaspoon cornflour (cornstarch), mixed with 1 teaspoon water
½ teaspoon liquid palm sugar (glossary), or shaved palm sugar (jaggery)

Among the hustle and bustle of Kampot's early-morning seafood market, I noticed a lady balancing two large, heavy baskets on both ends of a long bamboo yoke. She stopped in the live crab section and placed six tiny red stools in the sand, which were quickly sat on by hungry customers. When I went over to see what she was serving, she pointed and directed me to sit, then prepared a bowl of noodles within the minute. It was so simple, quick and light — vermicelli noodles, fresh mint, cucumber, bean sprouts, dried shrimp, fish sauce and peanuts, drizzled with thick coconut cream. It was divine.

METHOD

To make the sweet fish sauce dressing, pound the garlic, chilli, sugar and a pinch of sea salt together using a large mortar and pestle. Add the fish sauce and lime juice, mix well and set aside.

To make the thickened coconut dressing, heat the vegetable oil in a saucepan over medium heat. Add the spring onion and sauté for 30 seconds. Now add the coconut cream, cornflour mixture, palm sugar and a pinch of sea salt. Stir for 30 seconds, until the mixture comes to the boil and thickens slightly. Remove from the heat and set aside.

Soak the dried shrimp in a little boiling water for 5 minutes, then drain. Pound the shrimp using a mortar and pestle until it begins to break down. Set aside.

Meanwhile, cook the noodles in a saucepan of boiling water for 2 minutes, then remove the pan from the heat and stand the noodles in the water for 5 minutes. Drain well, rinse under cold water, then drain well again.

Divide the lettuce, bean sprouts, cucumber and herbs among four individual bowls. Top with the noodles, then the shrimp, then toss the salads separately.

Now add 2 tablespoons of the sweet fish sauce dressing and 2 tablespoons of the thickened coconut dressing to each bowl. Garnish with the peanuts and serve.

INGREDIENTS

2 tablespoons vegetable oil
2 garlic cloves, chopped
1 teaspoon Cambodian Chilli Paste (see Note)
30 g (1 oz) kampot green peppercorns (glossary), or fresh or brined green peppercorns
200 g (7 oz) baby squid, cleaned and skinned, cut into 4 cm (1½ inch) pieces, including the tentacles
½ onion, cut into wedges
¼ green capsicum (pepper), finely sliced
¼ red capsicum (pepper), finely sliced
1 long red chilli, sliced, plus extra sliced chilli to garnish
2 tablespoons oyster sauce
2 tablespoons fish sauce
2 teaspoons liquid palm sugar (glossary), or shaved palm sugar (jaggery)
1 tablespoon roasted crushed unsalted peanuts
60 ml (2 fl oz/¼ cup) coconut cream

WOK-TOSSED SQUID WITH KAMPOT PEPPER

SERVES 4

Kampot is famous for three things: crab, peppercorns and squid.
Their pepper is rated as one of the best varieties in the world, on par with Vietnam's 'phu quoc' pepper – so to cook it with fresh tender baby squid was just delightful. You don't need to wok-toss the squid for long, as it cooks very quickly. If you overcook squid, it just turns tough and rubbery. If you can't get Kampot peppercorns, regular green peppercorns will be an okay substitute.

METHOD

Add the vegetable oil, garlic, chilli paste and peppercorns to a hot wok. Stir-fry over medium–high heat for 30 seconds, or until fragrant. Add the squid, onion, capsicums and chilli and stir-fry for a further 1½–2 minutes.

Now add the oyster sauce, fish sauce, palm sugar, peanuts, coconut cream and a pinch of sea salt and stir-fry for a further 1½ minutes, or until heated through.

Garnish with extra chilli slices and serve.

NOTE

To make Cambodian chilli paste, soak 200 g (7 oz) seeded large dried chillies in 500 ml (17 fl oz/2 cups) warm water for 10 minutes. Drain, then squeeze out the excess water. Pound the chillies to a paste using a mortar and pestle. Add to a hot wok with 1 tablespoon vegetable oil and fry over medium heat for 3 minutes, or until fragrant. Allow to cool, then refrigerate in an airtight container for up to 2 weeks.

INGREDIENTS

375 ml (12½ fl oz/1½ cups) coconut cream
2 eggs, beaten
100 g (3½ oz) snapper or other firm white fish fillet, cut into 1 cm x 2 cm (½ inch x ¾ inch) pieces
8 raw small prawns (shrimp), about 150 g (5 oz), peeled and deveined
2 baby squid, about 125 g (4 oz) in total, cleaned and skinned, tentacles discarded, and the tubes finely sliced into rings
50 g (2 oz/1 cup) noni leaves (glossary) or English spinach leaves, torn
steamed jasmine rice, to serve

AMOK PASTE

2 tablespoons Cambodian Chilli Paste (see Note, page 218)
2 tablespoons Kroeung Paste (see Note, page 212)
1 teaspoon shrimp paste
2 tablespoons fish sauce
1 tablespoon liquid palm sugar (glossary), or shaved palm sugar (jaggery)

TO GARNISH

2–3 tablespoons coconut cream
2 makrut (kaffir lime) leaves, very finely sliced

Amok is Cambodia's national dish, served at most local restaurants in the country. Every cook has his or her own version, but this recipe was designed for the royal family. Traditionally, amok are steamed in banana leaf parcels, but you can also steam them in coconut shells, rice bowls or soufflé moulds. Noni is a tropical evergreen tree that grows about four metres tall. The fruit has medicinal qualities; the large green leaves have a nice lemon scent when cooked, but can be quite bitter raw. If you can't find noni leaves, use spinach leaves here.

ROYAL SEAFOOD AMOK

SERVES 2-3

METHOD

Bring water to a rapid boil in a steamer, wok or large saucepan that will hold a steamer basket.

Meanwhile, combine all the amok paste ingredients in a mixing bowl with a pinch of sea salt and mix well. Now stir in the coconut cream and eggs until well combined. Fold all the seafood through.

Line two or three small coconut shells or 300 ml (10 fl oz) heatproof moulds with the noni or spinach leaves. Using a slotted spoon, and reserving the spicy liquid, scoop the seafood into the moulds, over the leaves. Don't fold the leaves over the seafood.

Transfer the moulds to a steamer basket or bamboo steamer and set over the pan of boiling water. Pour the spicy seafood liquid into the moulds, reserving about 4 tablespoons.

Steam over high heat for 15 minutes. After this time, the mixture will have risen a little in the moulds, so use a fork to pierce a hole in each amok to deflate it slightly. Drizzle the reserved spicy seafood liquid over each amok and steam for a further 30 minutes, or until the mixture is set and has a light, soufflé-type texture.

To finish, drizzle a tablespoon of coconut cream over each amok and garnish with the makrut leaves. Serve in the moulds, with bowls of steamed jasmine rice.

INGREDIENTS

2 tablespoons vegetable oil
2 garlic cloves, chopped
2 red Asian shallots, finely sliced
½ onion, cut into thick wedges
1 tablespoon black or kampot peppercorns (glossary)
2 medium-sized blue swimmer crabs, cleaned and quartered
1 handful Khmer basil or Thai basil, plus extra to garnish, optional
1 long red chilli, finely sliced, plus extra to garnish, optional

TAMARIND SAUCE

125 ml (4 fl oz/½ cup) Tamarind Water (see Note, page 85)
2 tablespoons fish sauce
2 tablespoons liquid palm sugar (glossary), or shaved palm sugar (jaggery)

TAMARIND CRAB
SERVES 4 as part of a shared meal

Kampot has the best crab in the country; some say the best in South-East Asia. The most popular crab is blue swimmer, as it is more available and affordable than mud crab. I found their blue swimmer crabs quite small, maybe due to overfishing, but locals say theirs only grow to a certain size and are more tender than their larger cousins. They were right: I found myself eating right through their soft shells.

When buying tamarind, always go for the tamarind pulp that comes in blocks. Take it home and make your own tamarind paste or sauce. I never buy the paste already made in a jar, as I find it too light and artificial.

METHOD

Combine the tamarind sauce ingredients in a mixing bowl with a pinch of sea salt. Mix well, then set aside.

Add the vegetable oil, garlic, shallot and onion to a hot wok. Stir-fry over high heat for 30 seconds, or until fragrant.

Add the peppercorns and crab and toss for 7 minutes. Now add the tamarind sauce and cook for a further minute, or until the crab pieces are cooked through.

Add the basil and chilli, toss once and serve, garnished with more basil and chilli if desired.

THE QUIET SEASIDE TOWN OF KEP OFFERS VIEWS ACROSS TO THE VIETNAMESE ISLAND, PHU QUOC

People often ask how I come up with recipes on my travels. I simply ask the locals, and it is usually the elders who offer me the really authentic recipes. This one came from an 80-year-old man sitting on the side of the road reading his newspaper. He had a long grey beard and looked very wise, so I approached him and asked if he had an age-old recipe he could share with me. He stroked his beard, thinking for a few minutes, before telling me about this chicken dish, cooked in Coca-Cola. I had a bit of a giggle, as it didn't sound like an age-old recipe, but he explained it's a very popular country-style dish as all you need is a clay pot, a chicken, a few herbs and a can of Coca-Cola!

INGREDIENTS

5 cm (2 inch) piece of fresh galangal, peeled and finely sliced
10 makrut (kaffir lime) leaves
3 red Asian shallots, finely sliced
3 lemongrass stems, bruised
1 teaspoon sea salt
1 tablespoon oyster sauce
1 kg (2 lb 3 oz) whole chicken
1 tablespoon dark soy sauce
330 ml (11¼ fl oz) can Coca-Cola
ground white pepper, for sprinkling
Lemon Dipping Sauce (page 255) or lemon juice, to serve

CLAY POT COLA CHICKEN
SERVES 4–6

METHOD

If you can, use a large round clay pot – about 5 litre (170 fl oz/20 cup) capacity – for this recipe. You will need to soak it in water for 2 hours before using it. If you don't have a large clay pot, use another pot that is just large enough to hold the chicken, and skip the soaking step.

Combine the galangal, makrut leaves, shallot and lemongrass in a bowl. Add the salt and oyster sauce and mix well, then stuff the mixture inside the cavity of the chicken.

Brush the soy sauce over the whole chicken. Place the chicken, head down, in the clay pot, then pour half the Coca-Cola into the cavity. Now place the chicken breast side down in the clay pot. Cover the pot and place over a gas burner or charcoal, over medium heat. Cook for 30 minutes.

Turn the chicken over, then pour the remaining Coca-Cola over the chicken. Cover and cook for a further 30 minutes, or until the chicken is tender and cooked through.

Cut the chicken into quarters, then sprinkle with sea salt and ground white pepper. Serve with the lemon dipping sauce, or lemon juice for drizzling.

STUFFED KAMPOT SQUID

SERVES 4

INGREDIENTS

4 small squid, about 10-15 cm (4-6 inches) long, cleaned and skinned, reserving the tentacles
50 g (2 oz) minced (ground) pork shoulder
½ carrot, diced
1 teaspoon oyster sauce, plus 1 tablespoon extra
1 teaspoon sea salt
½ teaspoon fish sauce
½ teaspoon liquid palm sugar (glossary), or shaved palm sugar (jaggery)
1 spring onion (scallion), finely sliced
20 g (¾ oz) glass noodles
1 tablespoon vegetable oil
2 garlic cloves, finely diced
2 red Asian shallots, diced
4 snake (yard-long) beans, cut into 10 cm (4 inch) lengths
60 ml (2 fl oz/¼ cup) Sweet Fish Sauce Dressing (page 217)
2 tablespoons Fried Red Asian Shallots (see Note, page 155)
red flame flowers (glossary), to garnish, optional

METHOD

Dice the squid tentacles on a chopping board. Add the pork and carrot and finely mince together using a cleaver or two sharp knives. Transfer to a mixing bowl, then add the 1 teaspoon of oyster sauce, the salt, fish sauce, palm sugar and spring onion. Mix well and set aside.

Coat the squid tubes with the extra 1 tablespoon of oyster sauce and leave to marinate for 10 minutes.

Meanwhile, soak the noodles in a bowl of water for 10 minutes, then drain and cut into 3 cm (1¼ inch) lengths. Set aside.

Add the vegetable oil, garlic and shallot to a hot wok or frying pan. Stir-fry over high heat for 30 seconds, or until fragrant.

Add the pork mixture and stir-fry for 2-3 minutes, or until cooked, then add the noodles and stir-fry for a further minute. Remove from the pan and allow to cool.

Stuff each squid tube with the pork mixture, then close the end of each tube by stuffing it with four snake bean pieces, leaving half the snake beans sticking out of the ends, resembling a squid's tail.

Heat a chargrill pan or barbecue chargrill plate to medium. Chargrill the squid for 8 minutes, or until the stuffing is cooked through, turning the squid often.

Slice the squid in half crossways and drizzle with the sweet fish sauce dressing. Serve garnished with a sprinkle of fried shallots, and red flame flowers if desired.

Walking down Street 240 in Phnom Penh, I came across a store selling hand-made chocolate infused with Cambodian flavours: Khmer basil chocolate, honey sesame chocolate, ginger chocolate, and even Kampot pepper chocolate.
Sotherith, the lovely lady serving me, said visiting Kampot should be top of my list, as the squid there is extremely tender. She then scribbled a stuffed squid recipe on a piece of scrap paper, handed it to me and told me to try it out when I got there.
I promised her I would, and I'm so glad I did. It was just delicious.

CHAPTER 6

Vietnam
CHAU DOC TO BEN TRE

Vietnam
CHAU DOC TO BEN TRE

The Mekong River empties into the sea through the Mekong Delta in south-western Vietnam. The delta is known in Vietnamese as 'Song Cuu Long', or 'Nine Dragon River' delta. The Mekong helps form Vietnam's main agricultural and aquacultural region. It is the Mekong's busiest section, crowded with boats and teeming with life.

It was in Vietnam four years ago that I had the idea of filming a cooking series on the Mekong River. I spent a week with my family in Can Tho, enjoying their way of life, and discovering how much the people of Vietnam rely on this mighty river for their food and income.

I learnt that the Mekong starts its long life on the Tibetan plateau, then winds its way through China, Myanmar, Thailand, Laos, Cambodia and Vietnam. This great river is the source of nourishment and life for more than 60 million people in these countries. I wanted to follow this river from beginning to end, discovering the many different cuisines, cultures and landscapes along the way.

The Mekong Delta introduced me to many exotic ingredients in a short time. In one 24-hour period I ate fruit bats, coconut worms and coconut mice. Luckily, two out of these three dishes were really good!

After such a long journey along the Mekong, finishing up in Vietnam was a relief. I felt as though I'd arrived home. I thoroughly enjoyed being back among the cheeky, humorous ways of the Vietnamese people.

Mum and Dad met me for this leg of the journey, and I gained a little more insight into what the mighty Mekong gave to my family. We began our trip talking to the people of Chau Doc, about local foods and traditions. In Chau Doc we found a family who had been making and selling fermented catfish for decades, and I spent a day learning how to make the best roasted suckling pig in Vietnam.

We then travelled by boat to Cai Be, where I demystified the art of making netted rice paper, and spent an afternoon with my folks on a boat very similar to the one in which they had escaped Vietnam. It was the first time they talked openly about their experience on that tiny boat, en route to freedom.

My Greater Mekong adventure sadly ended in Ben Tre – although I am happy to say it was also where I became a true Vietnamese by eating everything that moves!

VIETNAMESE HOUSEBOATS HAVE LOW CEILINGS, SO EVERYDAY ACTIVITIES SUCH AS SLEEPING, EATING, WASHING AND CLEANING ARE CONDUCTED ON THE FLOOR

VIETNAM

Chau Doc, in An Giang province, borders Cambodia in the Mekong Delta region. It is near the picturesque Mount of Sam, where the Sam Mountain Lady is worshipped. This holy lady is known in Vietnamese as Ba Chua Xu Nui Sam. People travel from all over Vietnam to visit her.

The town of Chau Doc is well known for its fish, in particular catfish and mudfish. Locals ferment the mudfish in sea salt for many months, making a famously pungent preserved fish known as mam ca loc.

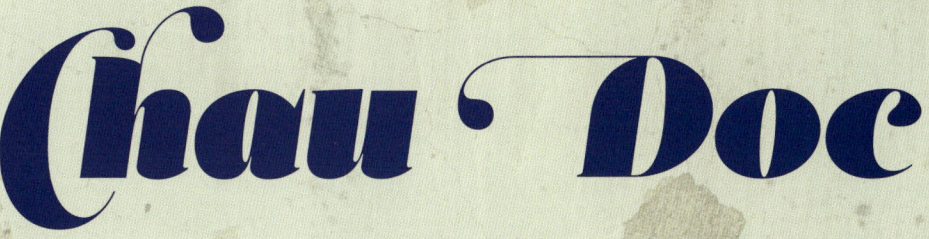

Chau Doc

Fermented mudfish may not sound that appetising but, like any food, you should try it at least once. My parents made many Vietnamese dishes using fermented mudfish when I was growing up, so I knew what it tasted like. But locals reckon if you haven't tasted Chau Doc's mam ca loc, then you haven't really had mam ca loc.

At the Chau Doc market I looked for a mam ca loc stall called Mam 55555, said to be the best in town. But it proved hard to track down. The market was filled with mam ca loc stalls, each one no more than two metres wide, and all selling the same varieties of mam. I asked four different stall owners, and all told me playfully that theirs was better than 55555. Strangely, it was a group of Japanese people who led me to the right stall. Many Japanese travel to Chau Doc to buy mam: like all fermented food, it has a 'umami' flavour – the elusive fifth flavour that the Japanese discovered.

The vendor was so delighted we came to her stall that she invited us home to meet her grandmother, who had perfected their fermentation technique. The proud grandmother shared one of her favourite recipes with me, a steamed Chau Doc style fish and pork terrine using a beautiful piece of mam. The terrine had a lovely savoury, salty taste, and a tongue-coating sensation: umami.

People from all over Vietnam make pilgrimages to Chau Doc to visit its many temples, especially Ba Chua Xu. They leave offerings of gold, money, jewels, clothing and, most extravagantly, freshly roasted suckling pig.

I spent half a day with the best suckling pig roaster in town, who works in a spectacular rustic kitchen, blackened from charcoal and fire. Mountains of wood were stacked high and beams of light shone through small openings in the roof, illuminating the smoke that lingered in the air. The pigs were slaughtered just before roasting, then marinated in a mixture of preserved bean curd, honey, five-spice, annatto oil and soy sauce. His was the most tender pork I've ever had, with a crispy crunchy crackling that I'll never forget.

INGREDIENTS

200 g (7 oz) mam ca loc (fermented mudfish; glossary)
400 g (14 oz) boneless pork belly, skin removed and the flesh minced (ground)
2 garlic cloves, finely chopped
½ teaspoon freshly ground black pepper
2 tablespoons caster (superfine) sugar
1 egg, beaten
2 red Asian shallots, finely sliced
2 egg yolks, beaten
coriander (cilantro), to garnish
1 red chilli, sliced, to garnish
steamed jasmine rice, to serve

Besides being the largest supplier of basa in Vietnam, Chau Doc is famous for its variety of fermented fish. It isn't only the Vietnamese who flock here to buy the pungent salty, 'umami' fish – the Japanese also travel here to take fermented mudfish back to their families.

Rows of fermented mudfish vendors line an entire side of the Chau Doc markets, with different varieties of the fermented fish stacked high on round plastic red trays. You can find fermented mudfish at your local Asian market in vacuum-sealed bags. This dish is quite pungent and salty, so it must be accompanied with raw herbs, vegetables and rice to balance it out.

FERMENTED FISH & PORK TERRINE
SERVES 4 as part of a shared meal

METHOD

Remove and discard the bones from the fermented fish. Dice the flesh and place in a mixing bowl with the pork, garlic, pepper and sugar. Mix together well, then stir in the whole beaten egg.

Spoon the mixture into a 600 ml (20 fl oz) glass or ceramic bowl. Sprinkle the shallot over the top, then cover the bowl with plastic wrap.

Half-fill a steamer, wok or large saucepan with water and bring to a rapid boil over high heat. Set the bowl in the steamer, then cover and steam for 30 minutes.

Remove the lid and plastic wrap. Pierce the surface of the terrine five times with a bamboo skewer, then pour the beaten egg yolk over the terrine. Cover and steam for a further 5 minutes, or until the egg yolk is set.

Remove from the steamer and garnish with coriander and chilli. Serve warm, with steamed jasmine rice.

The marinade for this dish was inspired by a suckling-pig roasting house I visited in Chau Doc. They receive 40 orders for their suckling pig each day. I spent half the day there to see how it was all done – and what an experience it was! The pigs are slaughtered, marinated, hung until the skin is dry, then roasted in enormous wood-fired ovens at insanely high temperatures for one and a half hours. It was the most tender pork I have ever tried, and the crispy crackling was just unbelievable. I am actually salivating just thinking about it.

INGREDIENTS

1 kg (2 lb 3 oz) pork belly, on the bone
4 cubes preserved bean curd (glossary)
1 teaspoon bicarbonate of soda (baking soda)
2 teaspoons cornflour (cornstarch)
1 teaspoon five-spice powder
2 tablespoons Annatto Oil (see Note)
2 teaspoons sea salt
2 teaspoons sesame oil
steamed jasmine rice, to serve
thinly sliced bird's eye chilli, to serve
light soy sauce, for dipping

ROASTED PORK BELLY MARINATED WITH FIVE-SPICE & PRESERVED BEAN CURD

SERVES 4

METHOD

Briefly dip the skin of the pork belly into boiled hot water, taking care to keep the flesh out of the water. Clean the skin by scraping the surface with a knife to remove the outer layer; the skin should be a consistent white colour. Wash the skin, then, using a large sharp knife, score the skin in either parallel lines or a criss-cross pattern.

Combine the preserved bean curd in a mixing bowl with the bicarbonate of soda, cornflour, ½ teaspoon of the five-spice powder, 1 tablespoon of the annatto oil and 1 teaspoon of the salt. Mash together well, then rub the mixture evenly over the pork skin.

In a separate bowl, combine the remaining five-spice powder, annatto oil and salt. Mix together thoroughly, then coat the pork meat with the mixture, massaging it in well.

Place the pork in a dish, then cover and marinate in the refrigerator for at least 1 hour, or overnight for a better result.

Preheat the oven to 250°C (480°F/Gas 9). Put the pork in a roasting tin, skin side up, and roast for 20 minutes.

Reduce the oven temperature to 150°C (300°F/Gas 2) and roast the pork for a further 10 minutes. Brush the skin with the sesame oil and roast for a further 20–30 minutes, or until the pork is cooked through.

Using a cleaver or large heavy knife, chop the pork into 2 cm (¾ inch) pieces. If your cleaver won't chop through the bone, cut the meat off the bones, then chop it.

Serve with jasmine rice, and small separate bowls of sliced chilli and soy sauce.

NOTE

Annatto seeds, also called achiote, add a golden colour to foods such as pork, chicken or rice. Annatto seeds and oil are sold in Asian and Indian food markets. If you can only find the seeds, you can use these to make annatto oil. Heat 1 tablespoon annatto seeds in a saucepan over low heat with 125 ml (4 fl oz/½ cup) vegetable oil. Heat just until the oil begins to shimmer; don't overheat or the seeds will turn black. Remove from the heat and set aside to cool, then strain the oil into a jar. It will keep for several weeks in a cool, dark place.

INGREDIENTS

500 g (1 lb 2 oz) basa, silver perch or cod cutlets
60 ml (2 fl oz/¼ cup) vegetable oil
2 tablespoons shaved palm sugar (jaggery)
2 garlic cloves, finely chopped
200 g (7 oz) boneless pork belly, finely sliced
200 ml (7 fl oz) young coconut juice (glossary)
4 spring onions (scallions), white part only, julienned
½ teaspoon freshly ground black pepper
1 red chilli, sliced

MARINADE

1 garlic clove, chopped
1 red Asian shallot, diced
1 tablespoon shaved palm sugar (jaggery)
2 tablespoons fish sauce
2 tablespoons oyster sauce
1 teaspoon sesame oil

CARAMELISED FISH IN YOUNG COCONUT JUICE

SERVES 4 as part of a shared meal

METHOD

Combine the marinade ingredients in a mixing bowl and mix well. Add the fish and turn to coat in the marinade, then cover and marinate for 10 minutes. Drain off and reserve the marinade.

Place a wok or frying pan over low heat. Add the vegetable oil and palm sugar and cook until the sugar has caramelised, stirring slightly.

Add the garlic and pork belly and stir-fry for 15 seconds, then immediately add the marinated fish.

Coat the fish with the caramel, then add the reserved marinade and cook for 1 minute.

Stir in the coconut juice and simmer for a further 6 minutes, skimming off any impurities that rise to the surface.

Serve sprinkled with the spring onion, pepper and chilli.

Basa is a type of catfish that is not too popular outside of Vietnam, as it comes frozen all the way from the Mekong Delta and it is really affordable – so it's perceived as being a cheaper, inferior fish. With this in mind, I travelled to Chau Doc to sample the fish fresh and judge for myself.
A local fish farm kindly gave me one to cook up, and I was pleasantly surprised: I caramelised the basa with pork and coconut juice and it came out wonderfully. It had very few bones and its white flesh had a light, firm texture that stayed very moist once cooked. If you can't get fresh basa, use fresh silver perch or cod instead.

TILAPIA FISH SALAD

SERVES 4 as part of a shared meal

INGREDIENTS
2 dried tilapia fish, about 100 g (3½ oz) each
1 tablespoon caster (superfine) sugar
1 Lebanese (short) cucumber, halved lengthways, then seeded and finely sliced
2 red Asian shallots, finely sliced
½ carrot, julienned
100 g (3½ oz) pork belly, cooked and finely sliced
1 bunch rau dang (bitter herb; glossary), leaves plucked
1 handful mixed mint, Vietnamese mint and basil leaves
1 teaspoon crushed unsalted roasted peanuts
1 teaspoon Fried Garlic (see Note, page 82)
1 teaspoon Fried Red Asian Shallots (see Note, page 155)
1 red chilli, sliced

SWEET & SOUR TAMARIND DRESSING
2 tablespoons Tamarind Water (see Note, page 85)
2 tablespoons fish sauce
60 g (2 oz/⅓ cup) shaved palm sugar (jaggery)
1 garlic clove, chopped
1 red chilli, finely sliced

My parents were looking forward to Chau Doc, as they'd heard of a special local medicinal leaf called 'rau dang'. These leaves are quite difficult to come across anywhere else in Vietnam, but their bitter astringency goes perfectly with this sweet and sour tamarind dressing. Look for bitter herb in your local Asian market, or simply leave it out. You'll also find dried tilapia at Asian markets.

METHOD

Combine the sweet and sour tamarind dressing ingredients in a bowl and mix until the sugar has dissolved. Set aside.

Heat a barbecue chargrill or chargrill pan to medium. Chargrill the fish over medium heat for 5 minutes on each side, or until browned. Allow to cool, then tear the flesh off the bones, discarding the bones. Place the fish in a large mixing bowl.

Meanwhile, combine the sugar and cucumber in a bowl and allow to sit for 10 minutes.

Squeeze the juice out of the cucumber, then add to the fish, along with the shallot, carrot, pork belly, rau dang and mixed herb leaves. Spoon over 1 tablespoon of the sweet and sour tamarind dressing and toss.

Transfer the mixture to a serving platter. Drizzle with another tablespoon of the dressing. Garnish with the peanuts, fried garlic, fried shallots and chilli and serve immediately.

VIETNAM

Cai Be is a town on the Mekong, criss-crossed with a network of smaller rivers and canals. Tourism hasn't boomed there yet, so you can experience the true essence of Vietnam.

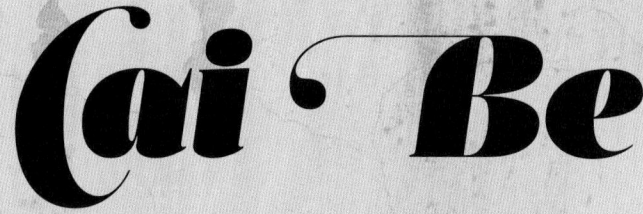

Cai Be

I was looking forward to arriving in Cai Be, as I love visiting rustic cottage industries to learn age-old techniques. It is important to visit these cottage industries to find out how things are really made. In the West we buy rice paper, noodles, tofu, fish sauce or coconut milk straight from a supermarket, but have no idea how they are produced, as they all come in a sealed pack, bottle or tin.

So all throughout this journey, I made a point to learn more about how these foods are made, as it makes us appreciate the product so much more.

Locals in Cai Be were more than happy for me to watch them at work. In one afternoon I saw sea salt being soaked, steamed and refined; rice and peanuts roasted together to make pop rice; young coconut water turned into caramelised sugar; ginger and coconut made into candy; rice made into vermicelli noodles; coconut flesh turned into jam; and most exciting of all, netted rice paper being made.

Six ladies sat on low plastic stools each with two small woks in front of them, and a large red bucket of liquid batter made from rice, salt and water. Their skill and speed was incredible. Watching these ladies at work, seeing them create perfectly round paper-thin netted rice paper in a matter of seconds, was like watching a live painting.

They used a primitive but creative tool to create the netted patterns: old aluminium sardine tins, with tiny holes drilled in the base. The runny batter was poured into the tin and held over a hot wok. The ladies worked their magic by moving the tin in a circular and criss-cross motion, to create a net of batter in the wok.

About 30 seconds later, they peeled the crispy rice paper off the wok and made another. If they were not fast enough, the rice paper would be far too thick. And for them, time was money – they got paid for every 3000 sheets they made …

INGREDIENTS

125 g (4 oz) snow peas (mangetout)
2 x 300 g (10½ oz) semi-ripe (but not green) mangoes, peeled and julienned
1 handful mixed mint, Vietnamese mint, basil and perilla (glossary) leaves, sliced
2 tablespoons vegetable oil
3 red Asian shallots, thinly sliced
3 cm (1¼ inch) piece of fresh ginger, peeled and julienned
450 g (1 lb) large raw prawns (shrimp), peeled and deveined, leaving the tails intact
juice of 2 limes

DRESSING

2 teaspoons dijon mustard
2 teaspoons rice wine vinegar
1 tablespoon vegetable oil

WARM MANGO & PRAWN SALAD

SERVES 4 as part of a shared meal

The French colonised Vietnam for almost 100 years, and the best things they left behind were their architecture, baking skills, beer, coffee and salads.
This is a great example of a dish that has both Vietnamese and French elements.

METHOD

Bring a saucepan of water to the boil. Add the snow peas and blanch for 1 minute. Drain, briefly refresh in cold water, then drain again.

Slice the snow peas lengthways and place in a mixing bowl. Add the mango and most of the herb leaves, reserving some as a garnish. Set aside.

Whisk the dressing ingredients together in a bowl. Season to taste with sea salt and freshly ground black pepper and set aside.

Heat a wok over medium heat. Add the vegetable oil and sauté the shallot and ginger for 3 minutes, or until caramelised. Add the prawns and stir-fry for 2 minutes, or until just cooked. Stir in the lime juice to deglaze the pan, then season with sea salt and freshly ground black pepper.

Add the prawn mixture to the mixing bowl, then pour the dressing over and toss until well combined.

Transfer to a serving platter, garnish with the remaining herbs and serve.

CRISP NETTED RICE PAPER FILLED WITH PRAWN & TARO

MAKES about 15 rolls

INGREDIENTS

1 egg white, lightly beaten
vegetable oil, for deep-frying
60 ml (2 fl oz/¼ cup) Nuoc Cham (see Note, page 258)

NET WRAP

500 g (1 lb 2 oz) rice flour
50 g (2 oz) tapioca flour
2 eggs, lightly beaten
1 teaspoon sugar
½ teaspoon sea salt

FILLING

100 g (3½ oz) minced (ground) pork
12 small peeled raw prawns (shrimp), about 100 g (3½ oz) in total, finely sliced
2 red Asian shallots, diced
1 taro, peeled and julienned
1 carrot, julienned
12 dried black fungus (wood ears; glossary), soaked in water for 20 minutes, then finely sliced
1 teaspoon sea salt
1 teaspoon ground white pepper
large pinch of sugar
2 egg yolks, beaten

METHOD

Place all the net wrap ingredients in a mixing bowl. Add 500 ml (17 fl oz/2 cups) warm water and whisk together until smooth. Allow to rest for 2–3 hours.

Combine all the filling ingredients in a mixing bowl. Knead well, using your hands, and set aside.

Heat a non-stick wok or frying pan over medium heat. Dip the fingers of one hand into the rested net wrap batter. Raise your hand out of the bowl, over a plate to catch any drips. Wait a few seconds for the batter to start running down in long dribbles, then drip the batter into the hot pan to form a round, lacy pancake. Allow to cook for a few seconds, then remove to a plate. Repeat to make about 15 net wrap sheets.

Lay a net wrap on a chopping board and scoop a heaped tablespoon of filling onto the centre. Fold the left and right sides in towards the centre to enclose the filling, then roll up from the edge closest to you, to form a neat, firm roll. Secure with a dab of egg white.

Repeat with the remaining net wrap sheets and filling, to make about 15 rolls.

Half-fill a frying pan or wok with vegetable oil and heat over medium heat, to 140°C (275°F). Deep-fry the parcels in three batches, first placing them seam side down in the pan. Cook each batch for 6–8 minutes, or until crisp, turning them every 2 minutes.

Drain on paper towels, then transfer to a serving platter. Serve hot, with a bowl of nuoc cham for dipping.

Making your own netted rice paper takes a lot of practice. I visited a netted rice paper-making house in Cai Be, where highly skilled ladies make 3000 papers each every day, using small recycled sardine tins.
They drill small holes in the base of the tin, then pour in the batter, holding it over a hot wok and moving it in a circular motion to produce a netted pattern in the wok.
If your rice paper nets end up too thick, don't despair – you'll find ready-made netted rice paper sheets at your local Asian market.

INGREDIENTS

500 g (1 lb 2 oz) rock salt
4 star anise
2 cassia bark quills
800 g (1 lb 12 oz) whole mudfish or barramundi, cleaned but not scaled

LEMON DIPPING SAUCE

2 tablespoons lemon juice
½ teaspoon sea salt
1 teaspoon ground white pepper

This recipe calls for a large clay pot, but if you can't get your hands on one, you can smoke the fish in another large pot or wok instead.
Cassia bark is also known as Saigon cinnamon. It is from the same family as cinnamon, but it is much deeper and more intense in flavour.

MUDFISH SMOKED WITH CASSIA BARK & STAR ANISE

SERVES 4 as part of a shared meal

METHOD

Pour the rock salt into a large clay pot. Arrange the star anise and cassia over the salt, then sit the fish on top.

Cover the pot and place over medium-low heat. Cook for 20-25 minutes, or until the fish flakes easily when tested with a fork.

Meanwhile, put the lemon dipping sauce ingredients in a small bowl and mix until combined.

Remove the fish from the pot and place on a serving platter. To serve, peel off the scales and skin and dip the flesh into the dipping sauce.

VIETNAM – CAI BE

VIETNAM

Ben Tre is another sleepy riverside town, known throughout Vietnam for its coconuts: it is surrounded by beautiful islands covered in coconut trees. Agriculture is also big here, in the form of sugar cane and cacao trees, along with exotic tropical fruits such as durians, bananas, mango, mangosteen and rambutan.

Ben Tre

My boat trip from Cai Be to Ben Tre was picturesque. I was here to visit family, who had been growing coconuts for 40 years. Times were tough, as the price of coconuts had plummeted, so now they use the entire tree. Young green coconuts were picked first and sold for juice; flesh from older ones was made into coconut milk, coconut oil, candy or desiccated coconut; and the empty shells were made into bowls, cutlery and handicrafts. The dried husks were woven into doormats and carpets: their biggest export.

To keep their coconut trees strong and healthy, growers constantly have to check for pests such as coconut mice and coconut worms. The growers tell me both these pests are delicious, so I decided to help them out. To capture the mice, an experienced climber clambers to the top of a coconut tree and shakes the mice's nest. The rodents leap out and people waiting on the ground gather them up. Marinated and barbecued, they are delicious!

Next we hunted down coconut worms. We found a tree that was already rotting away due to these little critters.

The men pulled out a whole handful from the trunk and dunked them in a bowl filled with fish sauce. They expected me to eat them alive! I've eaten a lot of crazy things on this trip – bats, rats, frogs, tarantulas, crickets, cicadas, cockroaches and snakes – but seeing these fat worms wriggling in the bowl was almost too much.

Then the men told me of a local ritual. I was to put a live worm in my mouth, let it move around a bit and wait until it bit me. Only then could I bite back and eat it. As I placed that fat slippery, milky worm in my mouth and let it wriggle on my tongue, I almost gagged. I was about to spit it out when it bit the side of my mouth, and out of reflex I bit it back and began to chew and chew. To my surprise, the flavour was like nothing I had ever tried before. I was expecting it to be slimy, creamy and rich, but it was the complete opposite: clean, subtle and light, like a piece of freshly caught and prepared kingfish sashimi. I was so impressed, I went back for another two. They gave me a pat on the back – I was a true Vietnamese man. It was the perfect ending to my two-year journey exploring the Greater Mekong.

INGREDIENTS

250 g (9 oz) heart of coconut palm
5 cooked medium-sized tiger prawns (shrimp), peeled and deveined
50 g (2 oz) cooked pork neck, finely sliced
1 small onion, sliced
½ carrot, julienned
1 handful mixed mint, Vietnamese mint, basil and perilla (glossary) leaves
60 ml (2 fl oz/¼ cup) Nuoc Cham (see Note)
1 teaspoon sesame seeds

HEART OF PALM SALAD

SERVES 4 as part of a shared meal

Heart of palm, or palm heart, is a versatile ingredient, which comes from the very tip of the coconut palm. The palm heart is made up of several young palm leaves that are still white and very tender. I've been adding it to salads a lot lately, as I love its light, almost sweet, flavour and its crunchy texture. Heart of palm can be served raw in salads, stir-fried or steamed.
If you can't find them fresh, they are also sold in glass jars at your local Asian market.

METHOD

Toast the sesame seeds in a frying pan over medium heat until fragrant. Remove from the heat and set aside.

Thinly slice the coconut palm heart lengthways and place in a mixing bowl. Add all the remaining ingredients, except the sesame seeds.

Mix well, then transfer to a serving bowl. Sprinkle with the sesame seeds and serve immediately.

NOTE

Nuoc cham is a popular Vietnamese dipping sauce. To make your own, combine 1½ tablespoons fish sauce, 1½ tablespoons white vinegar, 1 tablespoon sugar and 60 ml (2 fl oz/¼ cup) water in a saucepan over medium heat. Stir well and cook until just before boiling point is reached, then allow to cool. Stir in 1 finely chopped garlic clove, ½ finely chopped bird's eye chilli and 1 tablespoon lime juice and serve.

CHARGRILLED COCONUT MICE

SERVES 4 as part of a shared meal

INGREDIENTS

6 coconut mice, skinned, tails and feet removed, or 4 quails, cleaned and butterflied, but not skinned
1 tablespoon honey
1 tablespoon lime juice
1 tablespoon sesame oil
1 handful watercress sprigs, to garnish
1 handful mixed mint, Vietnamese mint, basil and perilla (glossary) leaves, to serve

MARINADE

4 cubes red preserved bean curd (glossary)
1 tablespoon sesame oil
3 teaspoons five-spice powder
1 teaspoon red curry powder (see Note)
1 lemongrass stem, white part only, finely chopped
3 red Asian shallots, diced
1 tablespoon diced garlic
2 teaspoons ground white pepper
1 teaspoon sea salt
1 tablespoon caster (superfine) sugar
2 tablespoons light soy sauce
2 tablespoons vegetable oil

LIME & PEPPER DIPPING SAUCE

1 teaspoon sea salt
2 teaspoons ground white pepper
2 tablespoons lime juice

METHOD

Put all the marinade ingredients in a mixing bowl and mix until well combined, mashing the bean curd as you go. Add the mice or quails, coating them well with the marinade. Allow the flavours to infuse for at least 30 minutes, or overnight for a better result.

Near serving time, mix together the honey, lime juice and sesame oil and set aside.

Mix the lime and pepper dipping sauce ingredients together in a small bowl and set aside.

Heat a barbecue chargrill or chargrill pan to medium. Grill the mice or quails for 3 minutes on each side, basting each side with the honey mixture.

If using quails, chop them into quarters. Arrange the mice or quails on a platter and garnish with watercress. Serve hot, with the dipping sauce and herb leaves.

NOTE

You'll find red curry powder at Asian food markets. It contains a blend of spices such as chilli, coriander seeds, cumin, lemongrass, galangal and garlic. Several different brands are available.

Coconut mice live up in coconut trees and feed on coconut flesh, so don't freak out – they are extremely clean and very tasty. While shooting my first cooking series in Vietnam, I had tried to catch my own coconut mouse, but failed miserably as they are just so quick. This time around, however, I succeeded – with the help of six experienced back-up men! If you can't get your hands on coconut mice, don't go eating the mice you find in your house or neighbourhood. Use quail instead.

MY JOURNEY FROM CAI BE TO BEN TRE WAS PICTURESQUE; SURROUNDING ISLANDS WERE COVERED WITH COCONUT TREES - THE MAIN LIVELIHOOD FOR LOCAL PEOPLE

GLOSSARY

Acacia herb (cha-om) A tropical member of the acacia family, much used in Thai, Cambodian and Laotian cooking. Fresh acacia herb has long, fern-like shoots, and an assertive flavour and smell that the uninitiated might find disagreeable; when cooked, however, it is delicious. It is sold by Thai grocers – ask for 'cha-om'. Out of season you can buy it frozen.

Asian celery Much smaller than regular celery, the leaves resemble parsley, and the thin stalks, which have a delicate yet fragrant flavour, are stringless and crisp.

Banana blossom heart The tender, inside layers of the young flower of the banana tree. It is available year-round from Asian supermarkets.

Banana trunk heart As the name suggests, this is the tender core of the trunk of a banana plant. It is a classic ingredient in the Myanmar dish, mohinga.

Betel leaves The glossy, heart-shaped leaves of a perennial creeping plant. Betel leaves are chewed raw for their mild stimulant properties, and used widely throughout South-East Asia in both raw and cooked dishes, most often as a wrapper for salad and other ingredients.

Bitter melon A popular Asian vegetable, also called bitter gourd. It is a member of the cucumber family, and both the leaves and fruit are used.

Black cardamom A large, black-brown pod with a camphor-like aroma, used whole as a spice. Its fragrance is also somewhat smoky, as traditionally it is dried over an open fire. The more common green cardamom pods cannot be substituted.

Black fungus (wood ear) Most commonly available dried, this Chinese mushroom is also called wood ear and tree ear mushroom, as it is said to resemble ears on the trees it grows out of. The dried mushrooms need to be soaked for about 20 minutes before using, and have a firm texture with a deep, earthy flavour.

Chinese cured pork A salted, dry-cured pork product, the finest of which are not unlike prosciutto or Spanish jamón. Either of these make fine substitutes.

Chinese red vinegar A rice-based vinegar, essentially the same as Chinese white vinegar, except for its rosy colour, which is usually attained by the addition of grains of red yeast rice.

Chinese white fungus A variety of fungus sold dried. It should be soaked before using. It has little flavour and a pleasant crunchy texture and is used in China in soups, salads and even desserts. It is believed to have high medicinal qualities.

Day-lily buds Also called golden needles, these buds are from a variety of day-lily flower and are used in Chinese cookery, in both fresh and dried form. You can use dried buds instead of fresh. These are easy to find in Asian supermarkets – simply soak them in water for 20 minutes.

Dried fermented bean curd Also called 'preserved tofu', this is tofu that has been air-dried and allowed to slowly ferment from bacteria present in the air. It is then soaked in water, rice wine, vinegar and chillies, or sometimes bean paste.

Dried shrimp Widely used throughout the Mekong River regions, dried shrimp is favoured for the special 'umami' or 'fifth taste' it brings to dishes. Dried shrimp is often soaked and/or pounded before using. It is easy to find in any Asian supermarket. Fresh prawns (shrimp) cannot be substituted.

Dried smoked beef Most homes in Myanmar have an open fire to keep the house warm, boil a kettle for tea and to cook family meals. People would hang beef fillets over the open fire for three weeks to smoke them. You may not be able to find this variety of dried smoked beef, so use beef jerky instead.

Dried tilapia This dried fish is only available along the Mekong River in Vietnam, where tilapia is found in abundance. You can use dried catfish as a substitute.

GLOSSARY

Dried tofu skin This is the dried skin that forms on top of boiling soy milk when making tofu. These skins are dried and sold as sheets or as bunched sticks.

Fermented soya beans Also called fermented black beans and salted black beans, these beans are made by two processes, firstly fermenting and then salting. They are an extremely popular ingredient in Chinese cooking. They are very salty, so a little goes a long way.

Finger root Also known as Chinese ginger, or by its Thai name, krachai, this rhizome gets its name from its unique, fingered hand shape. It has a mild ginger flavour. You can find krachai at your local Asian market in jars. Alternatively, substitute it with a little young ginger.

Fish mint Also called fish herb or chameleon plant, the leaves are green and heart-shaped, and the flavour rather bold and fish-like. Fish mint is often used raw in salads, but is also added to soups and used with grilled meats.

Ginger leaves In Vietnam, the fresh leaves of the ginger plant are chopped and added to dishes for the flavour they impart – a subtle ginger note that is far milder than the root. They are practically impossible to find outside of Asia unless you grow the plant; there are no real substitutes.

Indian root The Myanmar Indian root is also known as Japanese long onion, or naga negi. This Asian vegetable has a wonderful mild sweet, peppery flavour. It is great raw in salads, thrown into stir-fries or added to noodle soups. The green leafy parts are discarded and the long white stem is usually sliced diagonally.

Ivy gourd Often compared to bitter melon, the ivy gourd is the fruit of a vine. The fruits and young shoots are edible, but are best cooked and not used raw.

Kampot pepper The southern Cambodian region of Kampot produces pepper that is regarded as among the finest in the world. It comes in two forms: as fresh green peppercorns and dried black peppercorns.

Liquid palm sugar This is fresh sap, harvested from sago or sugar palms, and boiled. Most commonly palm sugar is available in dried form, as it is more convenient to transport. However, the fresh sap has a smooth syrupy texture, is easier to use and has a more subtle flavour.

Lotus flower All of the lotus flower can be eaten, including the flowers. The petals can be cooked or eaten raw as a salad ingredient or garnish.

Mam ca loc Mam ca loc is made of mudfish fillets that have been fermented in sea salt for 12 months. Unlike fish sauce, the fermented fish is used in cooking for its pungent flesh, not for its juice or water. When purchasing fermented mudfish, go for the variety that comes in fillets, rather than being ground.

Mam nem A sauce made from fermented salted anchovies, widely used as a condiment in Vietnamese cooking. It has a more pungent aroma and flavour than regular fish sauce. It is sold in bottles in Asian food stores.

Mam ruoc Vietnamese fermented shrimp paste, made from mashed marinated shrimps. The paste has an intense smell and flavour and is packed in bottles. You'll find it in Asian supermarkets.

Mustard greens Part of the brassica family, mustard greens belong to the same genus as the plants that produce mustard seeds, and have a similarly strong flavour. They are often preserved as a salty pickle, which is readily available from Asian supermarkets.

Noni leaves The leaves of an important medicinal plant, most commonly used as a wrapper for cooking and for flavouring foods, especially fish and meat.

Padek Also known as Laotian fish sauce, this traditional condiment is thick and pungent from fermentation. It comes in varying consistencies, with some varieties containing pieces of fermented fish.

GLOSSARY

Pennywort leaves Not all varieties of pennywort are edible. The edible Asiatic pennywort has slim, reddish stems and smooth, rounded green leaves. These are used in drinks, salads and cooked dishes.

Perilla Also called shiso, this highly fragranced herb is a member of the mint family. Its large, delicate, rounded leaves have a jagged edge, and can be green or purple. Perilla is used in salads and in a number of stews and simmered dishes.

Preserved bean curd A pungent condiment made by fermenting tofu. Not unlike strong, smelly cheeses in aroma and mouth-feel, it is packed in jars in brine and is either white or red. The latter is coloured with ground red rice grain, while the white curd can be seasoned with a variety of ingredients – chilli, sesame, anise, lemon, or even dried shrimp, for example.

Rau dang Also known as bitter herb, this strongly flavoured herb gets its English name from the literal translation of its Vietnamese name. Bitter herb has small, smooth, round leaves, with tender stems that are also consumed. It has long been used in Ayurvedic medicine for its medicinal qualities. You can find fresh bitter herb at your local Vietnamese supermarket; ask for rau dang.

Red flame flowers These bright red flowers belong to one of the most beautiful flowering trees in the world, also known as royal poinciana, flamboyant tree or flame tree, and related to the tamarind and mimosa trees. Its pretty flowers are edible and used in noodle salad dishes in Cambodia.

Red rice grain (hong qu) Also called red yeast rice, these grains are fermented with a particular mould that gives them a distinctive hue. The grains are ground, then added to meats or cooked dishes to give a rich burgundy-red colour.

Ridged gourd Also known as luffa, and related to cucumbers, ridged gourd is eaten widely throughout Asia as a green vegetable, mainly in soups and curries.

Sasbania Also called the hummingbird tree, this small tree bears bean-like fruit and flowers that are widely eaten as a vegetable throughout Asia. They are used both raw and cooked in curries.

Saw-tooth coriander (cilantro) Native to South America and related to regular coriander, this herb has a relatively large, oblong, bright green leaf with serrated sides. It has a much stronger flavour than regular coriander and is used in a variety of dishes – both raw in salads, and cooked in stir-fries, noodle dishes, soups and curries.

Shaoxing rice wine A famous sweetish Chinese cooking wine from the town of the same name in eastern China, near Shanghai. It is brewed from rice and is readily available from Asian supermarkets.

Sugar palm fruit As the name suggests, these are the fruits of the sugar palm; practically every part of this tree is used in some way or another. The fruit has a fibrous outer layer, which is edible, and a luscious, pulpy, juicy interior. Use tinned fruit if fresh palm fruit is unavailable.

Tempura flour A special low-gluten flour mixture (which sometimes contains baking powder), formulated for making the Japanese deep-fried dish tempura. It is favoured over regular flour as it gives a more delicate result in batters. It is sold by Asian grocers.

Vietnamese pickled ground chillies Known as 'tuong ot' in Vietnamese, this table condiment and seasoning is made of fresh chillies, ground garlic, salt, sugar and vinegar. It is widely used in dressings, dipping sauces, soups, salads and stir-fries. It is sold in jars and very commonly available from Asian markets.

Young coconut juice The clear watery liquid that develops inside immature coconuts. It is a popular drink and a commonly used liquid in cooking.

Young garlic shoots The leaves that shoot from a head of garlic, harvested for use while they are still very young and tender. They are popular throughout Asia as a vegetable addition to all types of savoury dishes.

INDEX

A
acacia herb 264
amok paste 221
annatto oil 241
annatto seeds 241
aromatic stir-fried smoked beef 98
Asian celery 264
Asian shallots, fried 155

B
baba 43
    traditional Naxi sweet baba 52
bamboo
    bamboo salad 104
    pork chargrilled in bamboo 117
    young bamboo shoots stuffed with pork & ginger leaf 97
banana
    banana blossom heart 264
    banana leaves 179
    banana trunk & chicken curry 131
    banana trunk heart 264
    chicken & herbs wrapped in banana leaf 58
    steamed fish in banana leaves 174
    steamed sticky rice cakes with banana 179
basa 242
bean curd
    dried fermented 264
    preserved 241, 266
beef
    aromatic stir-fried smoked beef 98
    beef wok-tossed in Lao whiskey 173
    dried smoked beef 264
    Khmer beef skewers 212
    Uyghur spicy beef skewers 24
beggar's chicken 43
Ben Tre 257
betel leaves 264
bitter herb 245, 266
bitter melon 264
black cardamom 264
black fungus (wood ear) 264
buffalo
    buffalo skin 153
    pork & buffalo patties with sticky rice 166
    warm buffalo skin salad 94

C
Cai Be 247
cakes, sweet coconut 180
Cambodia 190-1
Cambodian chilli paste 218
capsicums, chargrilled, stuffed with pork & Lao herbs 169
caramelised fish in young coconut juice 242
catfish 233
    tom yum pla soup with catfish 114
    wok-tossed catfish with galangal & green peppercorns 120
cha-om (acacia herb) 58, 264
chargrilled capsicums stuffed with pork & Lao herbs 169
chargrilled Chiang Mai pork belly 144
chargrilled coconut mice 261
chargrilled eggplant & prawn salad 72
chargrilled fish with crisp mint 45
chargrilled lemongrass tilapia 57
chargrilled salt-crusted lemongrass fish 156
Chau Doc 237
Chiang Khong 113
Chiang Mai 135
Chiang Mai noodle curry 141
Chiang Mai pork belly, chargrilled 144
chicken
    banana trunk & chicken curry 131
    chicken & herbs wrapped in banana leaf 58
    chicken stock 23
    clay pot cola chicken 227
    crossing the bridge noodles 23
    Ms Daen's Vietnamese/Lao ginger chicken 162
chickpeas: Shan warm chickpea 'tofu' noodle soup 91
chillies 125
    Cambodian chilli paste 218
    chargrilled fish with crisp mint 45
    chicken & herbs wrapped in banana leaf 58
    Thai chilli paste 123
    Vietnamese pickled ground chillies 266
    Yunnan chilli oil 33
China 14-15
Chinese cured pork 264
Chinese red vinegar 264
Chinese white fungus 264
clay pot cola chicken 227
clay pot fish 29
coconuts 257
    caramelised fish in young coconut juice 242
    chargrilled coconut mice 261
    coconut mice 257
    coconut worms 257
    heart of palm salad 258
    sugar palm with coconut milk 200
    sweet coconut cakes 180
    thickened coconut dressing 217
    young coconut juice 266
coriander paste 199
crab: tamarind crab 222
crisp netted rice paper filled with prawn & taro 252
crisp spring onion fritters 85
crossing the bridge noodles 19, 23
curries
    banana trunk & chicken curry 131

INDEX

Chiang Mai noodle curry 141
king prawn & tomato curry 76
rice paddy frog curry 123

D
Dali 27
Dali vegetarian rice noodle stir-fry 33
day lily buds 265
dip, spicy tomato, with raw seasonal vegetables 126
dressings *see* sauces/dressings
duck blood salad 155
duck-roasting 19

E
eggplant: chargrilled eggplant & prawn salad 72
eggs
　Luang Prabang salad 170
　red ant egg salad 187
Eight Dish Banquet 39

F
fermented fish & pork terrine 238
finger root 120, 265
fish
　caramelised fish in young coconut juice 242
　chargrilled fish with crisp mint 45
　chargrilled lemongrass tilapia 57
　chargrilled salt-crusted lemongrass fish 156
　clay pot fish 29
　fermented fish & pork terrine 238
　green mango & dried shrimp salad 196
　Inle stuffed fish 86
　Khmer fish salad 199
　mohinga 79
　mudfish smoked with cassia bark & star anise 255
　river fish steam boat 184
　steamed fish in banana leaves 174
　steamed fish with fermented soya beans & glass noodles 30
　sweet fish sauce dressing 217
　tilapia fish salad 245
　tom yum pla soup with catfish 114
　wok-tossed catfish with galangal & green peppercorns 120
fish mint 265
fish mint root & tofu salad 20
4000 Islands 183
frogs: rice paddy frog curry 113, 123
fungi
　black fungus (wood ear) 264
　Chinese white fungus 264
　lichen salad 36
　ox liver mushrooms 40
　wild mushrooms wok-tossed with cured pork 40

G
garlic oil 82
garlic shoots, young 266
garlic water 33
ginger
　ginger leaves 265
　Inle stuffed fish 86
　Ms Daen's Vietnamese/Lao ginger chicken 162
　young bamboo shoots stuffed with pork & ginger leaf 97
Golden Horse Gates 19
green mango & dried shrimp salad 196
green papaya salad 135, 137

H
heart of palm salad 258
hong qu (red rice grain) 266

I
Indian root 265
Inle Lake 81, 82
Inle Lake green tomato salad 82
Inle stuffed fish 86
insects 135, 205
ivy gourd 265

J
jackfruit salad, warm young 138
jaggery 200

K
Kampot 215
Kampot cold noodles 217
Kampot pepper 265
　wok-tossed squid with Kampot pepper 218
Kengtung 93
Kep 215
Khmer beef skewers 212
Khmer fish salad 199
king prawn & tomato curry 76
krachai (finger root) 120, 265
kroeung paste 212
Kunming 15, 19

L
Laos 148–9
Laotian fish sauce 183, 265
lap cheong 195
lemon dipping sauce 255
lemongrass 57
　chargrilled lemongrass tilapia 57
　chargrilled salt-crusted lemongrass fish 156
　steamed fish in banana leaves 174
lichen 36
lichen salad 36
Lijiang 43, 45
Lijiang cold noodles 46
lime & pepper dipping sauce 261

268　LUKE NGUYEN'S GREATER MEKONG

INDEX

lime dipping sauce 207
lime marinade 199
lotus flowers 265
Luang Prabang 165
Luang Prabang salad 170
lucky red braised pork belly 39

M
Mae Salong 125
mam ca loc 237, 265
mam nem 265
mam ruoc 265
mango
    green mango & dried shrimp salad 196
    warm mango & prawn salad 248
Mekong River 113, 149, 232-3
mohinga 66, 71, 79
Ms Daen's Vietnamese/Lao ginger chicken 162
mudfish, fermented 237, 265
    fermented fish & pork terrine 238
mudfish smoked with cassia bark & star anise 255
mushrooms *see* fungi
Muslim Chinese (Uyghur) 19, 24
mustard greens 51, 265
    one thousand layer pork belly 51
Myanmar 66-7

N
naga negi 265
Naxi people 43, 52
netted rice paper 247
    crisp, filled with prawn & taro 252
noni leaves 221, 265
noodle-making 27, 33
noodles
    Chiang Mai noodle curry 141
    crossing the bridge noodles 23
    Dali vegetarian rice noodle stir-fry 33
    Kampot cold noodles 217
    Lijiang cold noodles 46
    mohinga 79
    Shan warm chickpea 'tofu' noodle soup 91
    steamed fish with fermented soya beans & glass noodles 30
nuoc cham 258

O
one thousand layer pork belly 43, 51
ox liver mushrooms 40

P
padek 183, 265
palm sugar 195, 200
    liquid 265
pan-fried prawns with prahok rice 211
papaya: green papaya salad 137
Patuxai 153
pennywort leaves 266
pepper industry 215
perilla 266
pétanque 153
Phnom Penh 191, 205
Pi Mai (Laos New Year) 165
popiah skins 75
pork
    chargrilled capsicums stuffed with pork & Lao herbs 169
    chargrilled Chiang Mai pork belly 144
    fermented fish & pork terrine 238
    lucky red braised pork belly 39
    one thousand layer pork belly 51
    pork & buffalo patties with sticky rice 166
    pork chargrilled in bamboo 117
    pork laap 161
    pork stock 161
    roasted pork belly marinated with five-spice & preserved bean curd 241
    slow-braised pork hocks 132
    wild mushrooms wok-tossed with cured pork 40
    young bamboo shoots stuffed with pork & ginger leaf 97
prawns
    chargrilled eggplant & prawn salad 72
    crisp netted rice paper filled with prawn & taro 252
    king prawn & tomato curry 76
    pan-fried prawns with prahok rice 211
    prawn cakes 207
    warm mango & prawn salad 248
preserved tofu 264
Pu-erh tea 55

R
rau dang 245, 266
red ant egg salad 187
red curry powder 261
red flame flowers 266
red rice grain 266
    lucky red braised pork belly 39
rice
    pan-fried prawns with prahok rice 211
    red rice grain 266
    steamed sticky rice cakes with banana 179
    sticky rice 166
    toasted rice powder 187
rice noodles 27
    Dali vegetarian rice noodle stir-fry 33
    Lijiang cold noodles 46
rice paddy frog curry 113, 123
rice powder, toasted 187
ridged gourd 266
river fish steam boat 184

INDEX

roasted pork belly marinated with five-spice & preserved bean curd 241
Royal Project 125
royal seafood amok 221

S

Saigon cinnamon 255
salad dressing 36
salads
    bamboo salad 104
    chargrilled eggplant & prawn salad 72
    duck blood salad 155
    fish mint root & tofu salad 20
    green mango & dried shrimp salad 196
    green papaya salad 137
    heart of palm salad 258
    Inle Lake green tomato salad 82
    Khmer fish salad 199
    lichen salad 36
    Luang Prabang salad 170
    red ant egg salad 187
    tilapia fish salad 245
    warm buffalo skin salad 94
    warm mango & prawn salad 248
    warm young jackfruit salad 138
sasbania 266
sauces/dressings
    lemon dipping sauce 255
    lime & pepper dipping sauce 261
    lime dipping sauce 207
    nuoc cham 258
    salad dressing 36
    sweet & sour tamarind dressing 245
    sweet fish sauce dressing 217
    tamarind dipping sauce 85
    tamarind sauce 222
    thickened coconut dressing 217
saw-tooth coriander (cilantro) 266

seafood
    chargrilled eggplant & prawn salad 72
    crisp netted rice paper filled with prawn & taro 252
    king prawn & tomato curry 76
    pan-fried prawns with prahok rice 211
    prawn cakes 207
    royal seafood amok 221
    stuffed Kampot squid 228
    tamarind crab 222
    warm mango & prawn salad 248
    wok-tossed squid with Kampot pepper 218
seafood, see also fish
sesame seeds: tea-infused sticky sesame dumplings 61
Shan medicinal vegetable soup 103
Shan people 81
Shan warm chickpea 'tofu' noodle soup 91
Shaoxing rice wine 266
Shaxi 27, 36, 40
shiso 266
shrimp, dried 264
    green mango & dried shrimp salad 196
    mam ruoc 265
Shwedagon Pagoda 71
Si Phan Don 183
sichuan pepper oil 46
Siem Reap 190–1, 195
skewers 19, 183
    Khmer beef skewers 212
    Uyghur spicy beef skewers 24
slow-braised pork hocks 125, 132
som tum 135
soup
    mohinga 79
    Shan medicinal vegetable soup 103

    Shan warm chickpea 'tofu' noodle soup 91
    tom yum pla soup with catfish 114
soya beans, fermented 265
    Shan medicinal vegetable soup 103
    spicy tomato dip with raw seasonal vegetables 126
    steamed fish with fermented soya beans & glass noodles 30
    water spinach with fermented soya beans 208
spicy tomato dip with raw seasonal vegetables 125, 126
spring onion fritters, crisp 85
spring rolls, vegetable 75
squid
    stuffed Kampot squid 228
    wok-tossed squid with Kampot pepper 218
steamed fish in banana leaves 174
steamed fish with fermented soya beans & glass noodles 30
steamed sticky rice cakes with banana 179
sticky rice 166
stir-fries
    aromatic stir-fried smoked beef 98
    Dali vegetarian rice noodle stir-fry 33
stock
    chicken stock 23
    pork stock 161
Stone Forest 19
stuffed Kampot squid 228
suckling pig, roasted 237, 241
sugar palm fruit 266
sugar palm with coconut milk 200
sweet & sour tamarind dressing 245
sweet coconut cakes 180
sweet fish sauce dressing 217

INDEX

T
tamarind crab 222
tamarind dipping sauce 85
tamarind sauce 222
tamarind water 85
tarantulas 205
Tea Horse Trail 52, 55, 61
tea-infused sticky sesame dumplings 55, 61
tilapia, dried 264
tilapia fish salad 245
tempura flour 266
Thai chilli paste 123
Thailand 108-9
thickened coconut dressing 217
toasted rice powder 187
tofu
    fish mint root & tofu salad 20
    preserved tofu 264, 266
    tofu nwe 67, 81
tofu skin, dried 264
    clay pot fish 29
tom yum pla soup with catfish 113, 114
tomatoes 81
    Inle Lake green tomato salad 82
    king prawn & tomato curry 76
    spicy tomato dip with raw seasonal vegetables 126
traditional Naxi sweet baba 43, 52
tuong ot 266

U
umami (fifth flavour) 40, 237, 264
Uyghur people 19, 24
Uyghur spicy beef skewers 24

V
vegetables
    Dali vegetarian rice noodle stir-fry 33
    lichen salad 36
    Shan medicinal vegetable soup 103
    spicy tomato dip with raw seasonal vegetables 126
    vegetable spring rolls 75
Vientiane 153
Vietnam 232-3
Vietnamese pickled ground chillies 266

W
warm buffalo skin salad 94
warm mango & prawn salad 248
warm young jackfruit salad 138
Warorot 135
water spinach with fermented soya beans 208
wild mushrooms wok-tossed with cured pork 40
wok-tossed catfish with galangal & green peppercorns 120
wok-tossed squid with Kampot pepper 218

X
Xishuangbanna 55, 57

Y
Yangon 67, 71
young bamboo shoots stuffed with pork & ginger leaf 93, 97
Yunnan chilli oil 33
Yunnan province 15

Z
zheergen (fish mint root) 20

Series One crew, back row: Nicole Frisina, Luke Nguyen, Michael Donnelly
Front row: Wayne Hammond, Suzanna Boyd, Shane Brereton

An SBS book

Published in 2012 by Hardie Grant Books

Hardie Grant Books (Australia)
Ground Floor, Building 1
658 Church Street
Richmond, Victoria 3121
www.hardiegrant.com.au

Hardie Grant Books (UK)
Dudley House, North Suite
34-35 Southampton Street
London WC2E 7HF
www.hardiegrant.co.uk

All rights reserved. No part of this publication may be reproduced, stored in a retrieval system or transmitted in any form by any means, electronic, mechanical, photocopying, recording or otherwise, without the prior written permission of the publishers and copyright holders.

The moral rights of the author have been asserted.

Copyright text © Luke Nguyen 2012
Copyright studio photography © Stuart Scott
Copyright location photography © Suzanna Boyd

Luke Nguyen's Greater Mekong TV Series © Red Creative Media Pty Ltd, Special Broadcasting Service Corporation

A Cataloguing-in-Publication entry is available from the catalogue of the National Library of Australia at www.nla.gov.au

ISBN 9781742705125

Publishing Director: Paul McNally
Managing Editor: Lucy Heaver
Food Editor: Leanne Kitchen
Editor: Katri Hilden
Design Manager: Heather Menzies
Designer: Sarah Odgers
Photographers: Stuart Scott and Suzanna Boyd
Food Stylist: Sarah DeNardi
Production Manager: Todd Rechner
Production Assistant: Sarah Trotter

Colour reproduction by Splitting Image Colour Studio
Printed and bound in China by 1010 Printing International Limited